Praise for *If Truth Were a Child*

George Handley, one of the Latter-day Saint tradition's most gifted writers, desires to build a culture worthy of its revealed truths—and this work is a step in that direction. It is a searchingly honest examination of the disciple's quest, viewed through his own yearnings and failures—and small victories—along the way. A provocative call to the heart and mind alike.

—Terryl Givens, coauthor (with Fiona Givens) of
The God Who Weeps and *The Christ Who Heals*

In our rancorous era of polarization, *If Truth Were a Child* arrives as a breath of fresh air. George Handley calls us to a better version of ourselves, one characterized by capacious curiosity, serious moral engagement, compassionate critique, and most of all reconciling love. This is a wise and generous book that presents a model of being deeply Latter-day Saint in a pluralistic world, a vision that is both humanely religious and religiously humane.

—Patrick Q. Mason, author of *Planted: Belief and
Belonging in an Age of Doubt*

Drawing incisive connections between various aspects of Latter-day Saint life and thought that initially strike his reader as counterintuitive, Handley helpfully illuminates how Latter-day Saints today might live and believe with greater compassion, charity, and insight.

—Deidre Nicole Green, author of
Works of Love in a World of Violence

Handley's aim is to illuminate that vulnerable place where the human bleeds into the divine. To this end, he makes a strong case for why Latter-day Saints ought to pair a deep love for the humanities with an enduring faith in God.

—Adam S. Miller, author of *Letters to a Young Mormon*
and *An Early Resurrection*

This collection offers the thoughts of a generous and informed mind on big issues: why be a Latter-day Saint, what is criticism for, what do words mean, how to know grace? Readers will find themselves pausing to ask, What do I think about all these?

—Richard Lyman Bushman, author of
Joseph Smith: Rough Stone Rolling

IF TRUTH
WERE A
CHILD

A
Living Faith
Book

Living Faith books are for readers who cherish the life of the mind and the things of the Spirit. Each title is a unique example of faith in search of understanding, the voice of a scholar who has cultivated a believing heart while engaged in the disciplines of the Academy.

OTHER LIVING FAITH BOOKS INCLUDE:

Adam S. Miller, *Letters to a Young Mormon* (2nd ed.)

Samuel M. Brown, *First Principles and Ordinances: The Fourth Article of Faith in Light of the Temple*

Steven L. Peck, *Evolving Faith: Wanderings of a Mormon Biologist*

Patrick Q. Mason, *Planted: Belief and Belonging in an Age of Doubt*

Thomas F. Rogers, *Let Your Hearts and Minds Expand: Reflections on Faith, Reason, Charity, and Beauty*

Ashley Mae Hoiland, *One Hundred Birds Taught Me to Fly: The Art of Seeking God*

IF TRUTH WERE A WERE A CHILD

ESSAYS

GEORGE B. HANDLEY

A Living Faith Book

BYU
Maxwell
Institute

Cover illustration: *The Judgement of Solomon* by Hans von Kulmbach
Background: ilolab/Shutterstock.com and Lissabel/Shutterstock.com

The paper used in this publication meets the minimum requirements of the American National Standard for Information Sciences—Permanence of Paper for Printed Library Materials. ANSI Z39.48-19

ISBN: 978-1-9443-9473-8

Art Direction: Blair Hodges

Cover design: Heather G. Ward

Book design: Carmen Durland Cole

Printed in the United States of America

http://maxwellinstitute.byu.edu

Library of Congress Cataloging-in-Publication Data
Names: Handley, George B., 1964- author.
Title: If truth were a child : essays / George B. Handley.
Other titles: Living faith book (Neal A. Maxwell Institute for Religious
    Scholarship)
Description: Provo, UT : BYU Neal A. Maxwell Institute, [2019] | Series: A
    living faith book | Includes bibliographical references.
Identifiers: LCCN 2018046741 | ISBN 9781944394738
Subjects: LCSH: Christian life--Mormon authors. | Religion and the
    humanities. | Faith. | Church of Jesus Christ of Latter-day
    Saints--Doctrines. | Mormon Church--Doctrines.
Classification: LCC BX8656 .H39 2019 | DDC 261.5--dc23 LC record available at https://lccn.loc.gov/2018046741

For my students—past, present, and future.

Truth's value is manifest by the love we muster to build relationships in its pursuit.

Contents

Preface

I am a religious person. As a Latter-day Saint, I worship in church every week, serve in callings, and pray and read scriptures regularly. I am familiar with the Holy Spirit. I consider myself spiritual. I am also an intellectual. As a humanities scholar, I write and teach about cultures and engage in debate and research about ideas and values. I am familiar with philosophy. I consider myself rational. And yet I well know that for some my religious life can hardly be considered rational and that for others my intellectual life poses a risk to my faith. In these essays I would like to explore what I consider to be the seamlessness of humanities and belief, intellect and faith. To do this requires appeals to both reason and personal experience. Some of these essays are directly informed by my research as a literary critic, some less so, but any separation of scholarly and devotional thought would be artificial and untrue to my experience in any case. My thought and my faith have benefited both from each other and from my fortunate employment at Brigham Young University, which has uniquely encouraged and facilitated their integration. My objective, then, is simply to share what it has come to mean for me to think and believe as a Latter-day Saint. Our age is not one that is well acquainted with what it is like to inhabit faith, and far too many misunderstandings result. And I suppose too that behind my motivation is a persistent and nagging feeling that not only faith in general but my faith in particular is little understood in our culture today and that I will have dishonored my experiences by remaining reticent. I confess too that I am interested in providing a more rational atmosphere in which Latter-day Saint faith might flourish. It is sad and unfortunate that religion has ever pitted itself against reason or been falsely accused of doing so.

What keeps me in The Church of Jesus Christ of Latter-day Saints and what keeps me working at living according to its principles is the fundamental fact that I accept the tenets of my faith as plausible, compelling, and deeply moving. They make sense to me intellectually. More importantly, they have taken root in my very being as a result of acts of faith that brought personal witnesses of the gospel's spiritual truths. These started out as, and continue to be, attempts to make a go at being a Latter-day Saint, to "practice" the religion; that is, acts of conformity to what I understand to be the will of God, which then bring me gradually and consistently closer to God and make me happier in my life and more aware of the tangible and good fruits of faithfulness. I am speaking specifically of the many dos and don'ts of the religion such as Sabbath day observance, the law of tithing, the Word of Wisdom (no drugs or alcohol), sexual abstinence before marriage and faithfulness within marriage, dutiful fulfillment of lay responsibilities given to me in church, service to those in need, personal prayer and scripture study, and other important forms of spiritual discipline. I have never been perfectly obedient. What little I know I have learned not just from my adherence but also from my occasional deviations. There is a great deal I do not understand about the world and about my faith, but what I know is that I like the man I feel I am becoming when I take the claims of my religion seriously.

Belief and belonging are always precarious propositions, especially within an institutional context. I live with many questions. But I live in faith, which for me means that I trust that if I find myself at odds with the institution, in time I and/or the church and its culture will change and that a clearer picture will emerge. It also means that when institutional and social issues are a concern, I try to keep my focus on my commitment and devotion to Christ. I didn't choose the religion for cultural or political reasons in any case. I didn't choose it because Latter-day Saints are my tribe or because my identity is that of a Latter-day Saint. I chose it because I believe it. And believing it, I do what I can to help build a culture worthy of what I consider to be the religion's revealed truths. In the sincere hope that they are useful, these essays, however imperfect, are my intellectual and faithful offering to that end.

Some of these essays, as indicated in the footnotes, were previously published. In all cases, however, they represent my latest thinking on the topics. That is to say, in the case of previously published work, I have edited and revised with the goal of providing a collection that works better together as a whole. Like all writers, I feel that, as Moroni expressed so powerfully, "when [I] write [I] behold [my] weakness, and stumble because of the placing of [my] words" (Ether 12:25). My much stumbling inspires my gratitude for a charitable reader.

Why I Am a Christian

Being a Christian, as I see it, primarily means living in faithful relationship with Christ, a loving and divine personality and power. This relationship provides both motivation and capacity to change; peace in accepting what, for now, seems unchangeable; and a method for helping me to love myself and others more truly. To put it most simply, I am a Christian and strive to live a Christian life because doing so makes it possible for me to feel deeper joy and to express deeper love, beyond my natural tendencies.

I didn't come to faith first and foremost as a matter of taste. In other words, I don't recall that I thought things through and decided that Christ's teachings made the most sense to me. I didn't choose to believe in him on the basis of a rational decision, but on the basis of a series of experiences in the angst and struggle of coming to terms with myself that cast me upon his shores. It was more like the experience of falling in love, rather than, say, choosing a college or a career. I admit that this might not be helpful to those who wish to be persuaded of the rationality of Christianity before they are going to believe in it, let alone respect it. But living in Christian faith can make good sense to someone like me who feels a lack, a poverty, a hunger of spirit, and a profound sense of insufficiency and yet who also feels, or at least wants to feel, hopeful about what I might yet become.

The paradox is that nothing has exposed me to my own weaknesses as directly as my efforts to accept Christ and strive to do and become good. Seeing my weakness is the moment of truth, the deepest test of faith.

The paradox is that nothing has exposed me to my own weaknesses as directly as my efforts to accept Christ and strive to do and become good. Seeing my weakness is the moment of truth, the deepest test of faith. While discipleship certainly entails some victories in the battle against self, it also entails gaining the power to overcome the impulse for shame or to want to hide from others what I perpetually see in myself. In my experience, the path of discipleship is not a method of cloistering myself away from the evidence of my weaknesses but is instead a method for accepting and living with my brokenness, and hopefully becoming strong through it. My faith in Christ helps me see my failings more clearly, which is no small thing considering my propensity for self-deception, but it has also allowed me to feel real forgiveness and real power to move forward with hope.

So repentance is a way of life for me as a Christian. It gives faith a kind of integrity that is rare and precious and efficacious. As I age, the blessings of my efforts to repent with faith in Christ, however imperfect those efforts have been, become more apparent, and my previous impatience with myself for being too slow to overcome my weaknesses seems like so much wasted energy. I have never regretted any attempts to repent or to get up one more time after falling down.

We talk of sin as a deliberate rejection of God, but sin often feels to me more like being a slave to myself, unable to escape my own psychology, genes, upbringing, habits, or personality even and especially when I am aware that life calls me to better habits and deeper commitments. Maybe it's a paradox to describe sin as feeling trapped by genes and history, since sin is presumably the conscious choice of doing something I know is wrong, but often I do wrong even or especially when I wish or intend to do differently. In other words, sin is a bit like feeling divided, as if I don't fully know myself or feel capable of steering the ship I am on. I have never experienced complete freedom from such contingencies. I doubt it is possible to do so, and in some ways it might not even be desirable. I have learned over time that I would prefer to realize myself in my weaknesses and in the particularities of my life, not despite them. I want to have a new heart and to be a better person, but I don't want to be a different person, and I don't think God wants me to be either. He wants a better and more loving version of myself, but in my experience he seems to honor my experience in my moment and place on this earth.

Christ inspires me to try to love others, and then, in so striving, I find that my natural inclinations and affections prove insufficient. In this way he shows me my weaknesses. This is the bargain: I strive to emulate him, and he helps me discover in what ways I don't match up. But since his objective is not my despair but my happiness, he helps me see both what I am naturally disposed to do and also what is possible. My natural reactions to my weaknesses and to the weaknesses of others cause my love to flag, and there is the temptation to pull away, to judge, and maybe even to condemn either myself or others. Once I learned the way of repentance, however, after many years of repeated effort, I found that my despair at discovering my weaknesses was more readily replaced by hope. I am at the point in life where I can feel gratitude for my weaknesses.

Indeed, nothing has given me more confidence in the living reality of Jesus Christ as the Redeemer and resurrected Son of God than the way that my trust in him has converted my awareness of my insufficiencies into hope, into a palpable increase of love for myself, for others, and for life itself that is beyond my natural instincts. What sustains this love isn't willpower but the Spirit of God that rests on me when I seek him faithfully and honestly. I generally know I am not close enough to Christ when I do not feel unqualified love and forbearance and when I am full of complaint about my life. Bare existence is a tremendous miracle, a gift beyond proper reckoning. When I see my existence with gratitude, the simplest things bring the deepest joys and all of it feels enough for me. Christ's pure love, charity, transcends inclination and affections and starts to feel like a godlike appreciation for every person, every personality, each and every individual idiosyncrasy, and all the bare facts of geography and circumstance. In such moments, I want to love everyone and everything. Every person seems a miracle to me, every breeze, every mountaintop, every birdsong. But when that feeling of gratitude escapes me, I know I am distant from Christ's power. It is then that I must ask myself, Do I believe he can pull me out of the mire of my insufficiency? Will I allow him to make my weakness strong? Do I sincerely want to love, even if I don't yet feel sincere love? Self-pity, anger, and jealousy should have no place in the Christian heart. Neither should fear.

A willingness to repent and then to declare my faith has opened me to deeper appreciation for the meaning and power of Christ's atonement. I know the idea of declaring one's beliefs, especially Christian ones, is not all that attractive to some people. And I can surely understand the distaste many feel about witnessing, because it might seem like a kind of arrogance, but hedging my bets, fearing my own convictions, or perpetually hesitating will not give me Christ's strength to do his work. I must stand as a witness of Christ.

> I don't know that sharing belief has a high batting average for converting others, but when done in humility, it teaches oneself the shape and arc of love and something of the meaning of our universal kinship in the human family.

One day early in my mission as a young man in Venezuela I found myself looking down a dusty street filled with people, stray dogs, and the sounds of young children in the humid tropical air and feeling overcome by love for total strangers. I saw pain and aching hearts everywhere I looked, need in every human countenance, and I felt wells of pity and love for each and every one. It was an astonishing and sudden gift to feel such love. It may be regrettable that I had begun my mission without this kind of love already in my heart, but I hadn't yet been given that gift. I believe, however, that if it hadn't been for my willingness to repent and declare my beliefs, the gift of that love would have never come to me. I remember feeling surprised that I was capable of feeling so much love for so many and that it caused such profound joy. I have often since reflected on how rarely we see ourselves as truly belonging to each other. I don't know that sharing belief has a high batting average for converting others, but when done in humility, it teaches oneself the shape and arc of love and something of the meaning of our universal kinship in the human family.

While faith *in* Christ brings me into experiences with his love, faithfulness *to* Christ requires that I remember that love, learn to open myself to it, and give it generously to myself and others. Jesus's repeated calls for me to lose myself are calls to selfless orientation within the present world, to allow my ego and self-interest to be replaced with God's love for me and for others. As a Christian, I believe I have a duty to feel what others feel and to seek to understand the burdens of life as others experience them so that I might then begin the work of relieving those burdens if I can and mourning with others if I can't. Obtaining this kind of embracing and unqualified love is the objective, even if obeying and serving Christ and sharing my belief in him are the means.

Although this kind of love stems from my Christian belief and is motivated by a desire to assist others in what they can become, my Christian belief paradoxically requires me to love all people as Christ loves them, *as they are*. Indifference to others must surely count among the greatest sins for any Christian. My faith in Christ and in his gospel should make it more rather than less likely that love flourishes in my heart and in the world. Christian beliefs, simply put, should make a positive, palpable difference in my life and in the world. Discipleship is about seeing the countenance of Christ everywhere and seeing that my chances for good work in the world are never-ending.

Christ's pure love is not the same thing as blanket tolerance for all human behavior or belief. Love is tolerant, to be sure, but tolerance is possible without love since tolerance on its own does not even require knowledge of another person, investment of oneself, or risk of any kind. I am never certain how much tolerance or how much boldness to stand up for the truth I need in any particular situation. I am never sure I have struck the right balance. Being a Christian perhaps means being willing to live in this space of faithful forbearance and uncertainty. But I do not believe Christianity is ever an excuse for arrogance or for efforts to manipulate or control the choices of others, nor is it justification for feelings of judgment or condemnation or smugness

Because his call is for me to lose myself in service to others, it seems work enough for a lifetime just to follow the example and teachings of Jesus.

in being right. Christianity certainly transcends political parties and platforms. I squirm whenever I hear Christians describe how easily, in their view, Christianity translates into politics. I don't mean to suggest that Christianity should be irrelevant to policy, but I am rarely persuaded by Christian defenses of policy when they do not stem first and foremost from compassion, humility, forbearance, and love or when they seem more interested in negative protectiveness than in the proactive work of building a good society.

When I think about Jesus, I feel called to the work of relieving suffering, especially of those who are easily forgotten—the poor, the ill, the friendless and marginalized, those whose lives have been broken by circumstance and by harm done by others. I find it less important to expend my energies in worrying about salvation, because that leads to judging and condemning myself or others. Because his call is for me to lose myself in service to others, it seems work enough for a lifetime just to follow the example and teachings of Jesus. When I contemplate what Christ meant when he said "Where two or three are gathered together in my name, there am I" (Matthew 18:20), and when I think of the men on the road to Emmaus who discovered his presence in their midst as they walked and talked and ate together (Luke 24:13–32), I think the burden is on me to see Christ in the countenances of others, to see him in the mundane circumstances of my life. If all I see is weakness or insufficiency, it is not cause for despair but a challenge and opportunity to be met with the hope that is in Christ. William Blake said that "the tree which moves some to tears of joy is in the eyes of others only a green thing which stands in the way."[1] By seeing with the eyes of love, I can see the weaknesses in myself and others and understand them not as obstacles but as a cause for wonder that, human as we are, Christ remains among us, working, waiting, loving, and forgiving.

---

1. William Blake, letter to the Reverend John Trusler, August 23, 1799.

Why I Am
a Latter-day Saint

I didn't always believe in the tenets of my faith. As a Latter-day Saint, I came at them a bit as a contrarian. Sometimes that spirit of resistance is still in me, wanting to double-check things. I am most resistant when I sense that religious affiliation is nurtured more by coercion, intimidation, or other kinds of social pressure to be like-minded than by genuine conversion. I expect more from my religion than reinforcement of my predilections and preferences. Indeed, I worry when Latter-day Saint beliefs and practices feel too homogenous, too easily or coercively like-minded, or for that matter when good people leave because they can't tolerate the homogeneity.

Nevertheless, I am a firm believer. Rather than make a defense of the restored gospel per se and particular claims about the restoration of the priesthood and the translation of the Book of Mormon, topics about which much has been written and claims that I accept as a believer, I instead would like to focus on three aspects of Latter-day Saint belief and practice that are vitally important to my faith but that I find are often poorly understood. I am a Latter-day Saint because I am compelled by the importance of (1) personal revelation, (2) missionary work, and (3) temple work. These aren't so much arguments as they are ways of exploring and honoring what I consider to be vital gifts of the restored gospel.

PERSONAL REVELATION

To believe in something transcendent like a religion takes faith, but it seems that if there is no method of finding correspondence between that faith and what one comes to experience and to know, then one's faith risks becoming nothing more than an arbitrary and potentially reckless trust. I do not like the idea of believing in a religion unless there is some way I can genuinely know or have faith and confidence in its claims. I am a Latter-day Saint because of my experience with personal revelation, the method that the restored gospel places front and center as its promise to believers. A survey of the many instructions on revelation in the Book of Mormon and in the Doctrine and Covenants suggests that personal revelation is indispensable to discipleship. I love and honor this principle because of the way it shows God's respect for our agency, our conscience, and our potential for growth and change. When Joseph Smith entered the woods at the age of fourteen and sought resolution to his own conundrum about which church to join, he exemplified the responsibility of seeking personal answers from God. He wanted, as has every prophet of the church since, all members of the church to enjoy the privilege of their own access to revelation.

I have lived, like most people I suppose, with a desire for greater wisdom and understanding about ultimate truths and about the many difficult decisions I must make in the course of my life with regard to my family, my career, my friends, and my community. I am a Latter-day Saint because answers have come to me about a variety of questions I have posed in prayer, questions about whether or not God is there and is listening, about whether or not Christ is the Redeemer, about whether or not the Book of Mormon is the word of God, and about whether or not I should dedicate my life to service in the church. In each case over time, I have felt increasingly strong answers in the affirmative. I am more confident than ever that this process is ongoing

I expect more from my religion than reinforcement of my predilections and preferences. Indeed, I worry when Latter-day Saint beliefs and practices feel too homogenous, too easily or coercively like-minded, or for that matter when good people leave because they can't tolerate the homogeneity.

and can lead to ever greater levels of understanding and sacred knowledge. My understanding of personal revelation is itself a work in progress, but I do insist on its central value to my life as a Latter-day Saint.

From personal experience, I have learned that the Lord grants me higher understanding to the degree I am willing to improve my life and rethink my assumptions. Revelation, in other words, is never independent of my willingness to change. It is both the result of and a catalyst for repentance. Jesus taught, "If ye continue in my word, . . . ye shall know the truth, and the truth shall make you free" (John 8:31–32). Alma taught that the plan of salvation is vital knowledge, but he asks: "What natural man is there that knoweth these things? I say unto you, there is none that knoweth these things, save it be the penitent" (Alma 26:21). If revelation always came directly in line with our expectations and never seemed to require any change, then I don't suppose we could call it revelation at all, because it would be indistinguishable from the result of human deliberation, casting a vote, and exercising our will. While such deliberation is essential to reaching greater understanding in a secular and democratic society, in the church we seek revelation by combining such reasoning and desire with faith in the Lord's capacity to steer us aright.

Faced with uncertainty and unanswered questions, we may be tempted to grow impatient with God. The scriptures praise those that "wait upon the Lord" (Isaiah 40:31). In my experience, the waiting eventually provokes an honest examination of my life, and when I begin to imagine why I might need to repent and ask a different question or to live with different priorities, I find that God seems the most willing to reveal something new to me. He seems, in short, more interested in shaping me than he is in directing the course of my life. Because revelations about what I should do with my life and how I should live come more easily than revelations about what I should know, I suspect that knowing the will of the Lord is more to be desired than knowing the mind of the Lord. Besides, eternal truth isn't just information; it is an understanding that is the fruit of a dynamic, evolving relationship with divine love. I believe there is a risk that in all our emphasis on testimony, we might fetishize knowledge apart from relationships and apart from character.

One crucial experience taught me this lesson. As soon as I assumed my first position as an assistant professor in Arizona, I had the distinct feeling that I should learn as much as I could while I lived there even though I suspected that I wouldn't be there for very long. At the time, I assumed this was because my destiny was to be on the East Coast at a prestigious school. That was my desire, in any case. But as I began the application process to several schools, the doors to those opportunities were closed one by one, except for one school: Brigham Young University. Offered a job there, I began the process of obtaining an answer about whether or not I should accept it. I knew the decision would have enormous consequences for my children, and my wife Amy and I spent a long time on our knees, at the temple, and in discussion with one another, unable to feel right about it. Finally, we had a talk about our attitude. We both discovered that maybe we were worrying too much about what kind of neighborhood we would live in or what kind of schools our kids would go to and not taking enough responsibility for the kind of environment we provided in the home. I felt a distinct need to repent of this prejudicial attitude before the Lord would be willing to reveal his will. I could see that we needed a more portable home life, one that we took more responsibility for, and a more generous desire to see the good in others, no matter where we lived. I pleaded with the Lord for forgiveness for the impure motives that had informed my question, and finally, after a fast, I knelt and asked the Lord again if we should go to BYU. A clear and reassuring feeling came over me that we should go. Amy came to a similar resolution.

I sometimes hear my fellow Latter-day Saints say that the scriptures and the gospel can provide all the answers to life's questions. I believe the scriptures provide the most essential answers to life and are almost inexhaustible as a resource for inspiration when we read with real hunger. But I am not sure I would claim they have all the answers. First, as the ninth article of faith makes clear, the Lord will "yet reveal many great and important things pertaining to the Kingdom of God." The Book of Mormon itself, the single greatest act of restoration in the latter days, points to "other books" and future revelations yet to be revealed (1 Nephi 13:39). And second, by so insisting, we might risk trivializing how long and drawn out and sometimes difficult it is to get answers to certain questions, and we might then miss the deeper and more valuable purpose of such striving and waiting. If we make revelation sound easy, we set ourselves up for impatience and disillusionment. I do not believe, in other words, that personal revelation is always automatic, and I would go so far as to say that I am a Latter-day Saint both because the Lord has answered my prayers about my fundamental commitments and because he doesn't answer all my questions, at least not right away or in the way I hope. Besides, revelation isn't just about answers; it is sometimes a means of teaching us strength and wisdom and integrity. I don't even know why I would want to believe that a religion should provide all the answers of life. How else would I develop faith or be stretched to grow spiritually? Where would be the cause for wonder? Why would I want to believe in a revelatory process that shames or obviates the need of my own reasoning, my life experiences, and my personality? The fact that the Lord provides answers but not all of them doesn't mean we aren't led by the Lord or that we should ever stop trying to be led by him, but it does mean we should be careful not to assume that when a revelation comes, we now know more than we in fact do.

There is one answer, however, I always get when I pray with sincerity and humility, and that is that the Lord hears me, that he is with me, and that he will give me the power and love to sustain me in times of trial and difficulty. Because of the way this changes me for the better, such revelations of God's love have proved to be more valuable than a direct answer to my specific questions. The Lord seems to want me to persist in loving, trusting, and growing; and by not answering all my questions right away or according to my desires, he invites me to grow toward him in a way I otherwise wouldn't feel inclined to if everything came easily, immediately, or as expected. To speak of God as a kind of divine Siri, Google search, or vending machine is to rob us of a relationship with a living and loving divine being. I worry that if we trivialize revelation in this way, members will become disillusioned when revelation proves harder to come by. Besides, if it took King Lamoni's father a willingness to give up half of his kingdom and all of his sins to know God (Alma 20:23; 22:16–18), why should I assume it will be far easier for me to search and find God?

As I learned in my prayer about moving to BYU, if I focus too much on an answer to my question and compartmentalize revelation too narrowly, I miss revelations about life in its fullest range of experiences. It took a long time to learn that prayer is not only a request. It is a chance for recognition of God, even

When I feel God's love most deeply and strongly, I feel as if revelation is what it means simply to be alive and full of wonder.

praise. Just thanking God or pleading for more spirit and more love has opened my eyes more to God's glory around me and taught me that God's illuminating light is more or less like the sunshine: it is ubiquitous and always present, informing the shape of all things and giving life to all it touches, even though at times it is shrouded by circumstance where it gives meaning to the temporary darkness. When God reveals his Spirit and his love to me, it changes how I view this world. This is when I begin to understand what Christ meant when he commanded us to pray always. The earth and its myriad and marvelous forms seem aflame with God's glory, and I can more readily identify his hand in inspired religions; inspired works of literature, music, and art; and examples of godly service in every culture on earth. When I feel God's love most deeply and strongly, I feel as if revelation is what it means simply to be alive and full of wonder. Walking in this kind of light, one realizes that God is more with us, more involved in our internal conversation with ourselves, and more involved in the mystery and wonder of our existence than we might have realized. There is probably some risk, then, in overthinking revelation and assuming it is some kind of highly specialized and coded transmission of information, since we might miss the most basic manifestations of God's love, the joy of loving relationships, and the wonder of existence itself.

Sometimes when I have prayed with great difficulty in times of sorrow and trial, feelings of peace and comfort have swept over me as if I were being embraced. I have prayed for knowledge and understanding of spiritual matters, and answers have come in the form of sudden moments of clarity and understanding, either immediately during a prayer or sometime afterward. Other revelations have come in the form of experiences that have provided deeper wisdom about situations or conundrums in my life. Many times I have felt an increased capacity and strength to love and to endure when the specific answer I have sought hasn't come. On a few very special occasions in my life, these revelations have come in the form of dreams from which I have awakened with a paradigm-shifting sense of how I ought to live my life. I would say revelation comes to me very often while reading great books or listening to great music or watching an inspired movie. And it comes most easily on a mountain trail or in the celestial room of the temple, where I feel most attuned to God's creations. These moments are a source of great comfort to me and a reason for my abiding love for great art and for nature. And finally, whenever I struggle to feel God near me and his reality seems to drift, I am always amazed at how quickly a spirit of love and confidence and optimism comes to me when I earnestly study God's word and simply and directly ask the Lord whom I might be able to serve. Names and faces and ideas come to me right away, and when I act on those impressions, I am immediately drawn closer to God and my confidence is strengthened. This seems as great an evidence as any that God lives and loves me.

What I really mean to say is that I like the Latter-day Saint understanding of personal revelation that gives me responsibility for what I believe. Since knowledge cannot be separated from character, how I live affects the shape and mood and vitality of my beliefs more directly than almost anything else. Precisely because of the way revelations have invited me to change and seem to be facilitated by the changes I have made, my confidence in the truths of the restored gospel has grown. Knowledge of the truth, to put it simply, is never independent of what I am willing to do with that knowledge. In this way spiritual learning seems different from other kinds of learning. I might be able to master algebra or a foreign language or the chemistry tables without love and humility in my heart, but my capacity for spiritual learning is directly affected by my desire to be corrected. I have learned that it is simply too easy to slip into self-justifications. For that reason I am suspicious of claims that one ought to live one's life merely and only according to one's conscience. I certainly believe in the importance of integrity and being true to oneself, but having a flawed character ever in need of further reformation, I feel some caution about trusting my own conscience above all else. As I read the first section of the Doctrine and Covenants, my belief in continual and personal revelation helps me avoid the trap of worshipping a God after my own image, shaped according to my own imperfect judgment.

In other words, personal revelation provides me a reliable method for checking in from time to time to make sure that my convictions, the lights by which I guide myself, are as close to God's truths as they can be. That method involves close reading of scripture, close attention to the teachings of living prophets and apostles who lead my church, and a community conversation with friends and members who most immediately surround me. For me, revelation is both personal *and* continuing and, as a process, should be both individual *and* corporate, that is, collectively embedded in our membership in the body of faith. I receive revelation not only alone but also in a community, and

> If personal revelation is possible,
> it is also possible for all people,
> and that means I should be as eager
> to hear God's voice in the privacy
> of my own prayers as I am about
> hearing it in the voices of others.
> And I should also strive to be
> that kind of voice for others.

that is probably because it would be selfish to believe that revelation was for me alone. If personal revelation is possible, it is also possible for all people, and that means I should be as eager to hear God's voice in the privacy of my own prayers as I am about hearing it in the voices of others. And I should also strive to be that kind of voice for others. I am instructed each and every Sunday by God through very human and particular personalities. Not long ago in sacrament meeting a very young boy boldly stood and talked about the blessing of having choices in life. As I listened, all I could think about was that if God was desirous to say anything to us as a ward that morning, it would be exactly what that boy, with his frail and small voice, was saying. And when I have listened to the prophets and apostles of my church, I have frequently had that same feeling that God is speaking through them on behalf of all of us. While listening to these special witnesses, if I am willing to ask myself, "What does Christ seem to be asking of me now?" I find myself able to better discern that portion of God's will to which they are giving voice.

The corporate nature of this enterprise often creates challenges, but those challenges provide one of the restored gospel's greatest blessings. It means checking ourselves against people whose personalities and worldviews don't match ours exactly. This can result in turbulence and conflict, but in such moments I remind myself that it would be a contradiction to insist on and believe in personal revelation and then be categorically dismissive or distrustful of claims to inspiration by others. And if I believe revelation is possible for others too, it also means revelation is never complete, including my own, and that difference of opinion, even on sacred matters, is likely, maybe even inevitable. This makes dialogue and collaboration necessary to further winnow and refine truth, which is to say we need each other. For this reason I never stop asking questions, and I don't believe my loyalty to the body of the church requires me to give up my search for truth. Quite the opposite. Revelation doesn't have its fullest meaning unless it is deeply processed and ratified throughout the body of believers. In the church we are unified by the trust that God can speak to us collectively and individually, but our unity becomes the most meaningful and sustainable when we give ourselves and others the time and space to work out our own individual relationship to the word. I believe it is lack of faith that causes us to feel impatient with and intolerant of the inevitable variety of experiences with faith in any family or church community. Unity achieved through coercion and intimidation is not unity but a cheap and false conformity.

Today there is great cynicism about revelation in and outside the church. While I find wariness about coercion understandable, I believe the cynical reactions to oversimplified understandings of revelation to be equally oversimplified. I don't always understand how I should feel about every controversy or doctrine, but it is not hard to receive revelation about what I should think of Christ or how I ought to be living my life. That is no small matter, and I am indebted beyond words for it. I would even say that the stronger my fidelity to the practices of my religion, the greater the confidence I feel about the truthfulness of the restored gospel and my role in it and the freer my intellect feels to explore, ask questions, and turn over new soils.

MISSIONARY WORK

When I came home from my mission and returned to Stanford University, some students and professors questioned my right to go to another part of the globe and announce that I had the truth and others did not. I think that had to do with certain suspicions about the presumption and arrogance of such an enterprise. It was hard to explain myself to their satisfaction. The truth is that I was terrified when I arrived in Venezuela, and I doubted my purpose and presence there many times, especially early on. The culture, the language, and the context were often overwhelming and crushing in their powers of disorientation. I remember teaching an older woman about the story of Joseph Smith in my first week in Venezuela. She didn't have to let us into her home, but she did. She was bored with us, and in the end our story held no interest for her. I remember feeling that the earth beneath me was shaking and might swallow me up. What was I doing here? Why had I come all this way believing that this story would matter? And suddenly my own belief in my religion seemed to collapse into nothing more than an inflated confidence in my ethnic story as a Latter-day Saint.

But I had had experiences that had convinced me that Joseph's story was more than my ethnic story, that the importance of my religion had less to do with me and more to do with God and with others. I knew my faith needed to be more than a self-centered conviction, that it needed to be stripped of my own biases and predilections. So I kept trying to remain focused on the universals of my religion, and not merely on my personal understanding of it, and to teach with sincere love. Slowly and miraculously, I started to find people who wanted to listen, who indeed seemed hungry to hear, and who happily joined the church and changed their lives for the better. I can't count the number of miracles I witnessed in those two years.

It is fair to ask why a religious conviction needs to be expressed and shared publicly. Why can't it simply be a private and personal matter? Given the world's long history of religious intolerance and violence, it would seem to be a safer bet to stay at home and stay quiet about religious convictions. I have spent a great deal of my education learning about the pitfalls of religious intolerance, and I have been pained beyond my capacity to express by the atrocities of violence that have been done in the name of Christ and of other religions. I want no truck with violent and intolerant forms of Christianity, or of any other religious tradition for that matter. I find them morally repulsive, and I refuse to believe they are pleasing to God. I think it is fair and right to expect that religious people who wish to share their convictions show awareness of and sensitivity about that history and that they undertake the task of sharing their beliefs with appropriate humility and respect for all people. But I also think that when people come to accept the universality of a religion (in my case the divine mission of Jesus Christ as the Redeemer of the world and the restoration of his gospel), it is logical for them to wish to share their convictions; and it is fair, I believe, to allow them that freedom. Such effort gives belief much needed integrity and honesty. The fact that The Church of Jesus Christ of Latter-day Saints is so determined to declare its beliefs to the world can sometimes turn people away from it, but if a religion has any claim to truth, wouldn't we expect and even want it to be shared? The importance of missionary work is one reason why I am a Latter-day Saint.

And let's be clear: there is a difference between violence, intolerance, and manipulation and honest sharing of what one has witnessed and experienced and hopes to be of spiritual worth for others. Too often today we hear criticism of religious conviction as if it were already guilty of such sins simply by virtue of being announced. It doesn't help that some religiously outspoken people are embarrassingly intolerant and uncharitable in their views of others, but it is also true that we don't seem to think very clearly anymore in our culture about religion. Religion is too easily dismissed and too flatly equated with intolerance. This seems especially unfair considering there doesn't seem to be the same standard of suspicion applied to secular convictions expressed in the public square. All beliefs and convictions must have to answer for themselves in the public and plural space of the civic sphere, but that is all the more reason to allow and respect the freedom to share belief.

I respect and admire those who share their beliefs with others, whether those beliefs come from other religions or from secular views. Some religious people look down on secular humanitarian work, as if it were less important or motivated by shortsighted goals. I don't share those views. Some secular people look down on the work of missionaries as meaningless or foolish because it is based on unprovable metaphysical claims. I don't share those views either. I think any work that seeks and effectually manages to improve human life and human happiness, that alleviates suffering, and that requires deeper selflessness is God's work. I learned to admire a great many of my secular friends at Stanford and later at Berkeley who devote their whole lives to living for a purpose they believe in with all their hearts and who share openly and publicly their convictions in the hope that others might join in. There are those who fight against political oppression, those who fight against poverty and illness, those who fight for human rights and for the environ-

> ## Religion is too easily dismissed and too flatly equated with intolerance. This seems especially unfair considering there doesn't seem to be the same standard of suspicion applied to secular convictions expressed in the public square.

ment and for education. They inspire me, and I share many of those same convictions because of, not in spite of, my religious beliefs. But I also believe that important motivations and aspirations of a spiritual nature should inform our approach to the world's problems and that spiritual truth can provide a kind of healing that is just as important as the physical alleviation of suffering.

I do not understand a religion that believes in its own universality but does not have an intention or even a method for sharing its message with others. That seems to risk a kind of strange narcissism, as if to say, "We are right about the world, but the rest of the world is just out of luck." Feeling chosen or called by God should not be equated with membership in an elite club. Rather, it bestows a responsibility to extend God's blessings to others. We are all God's children, and so belonging to a universal religion means shedding one's own self-interest and striving to promote the welfare of all, not just those in one corner or tribe. It makes little sense for me to claim I believe in Christ but then refuse to engage in the work of sharing his story and teachings and serving others as he did.

The aspiration to take the good news of Christ to everyone involves exposing oneself to real risk—the risk of being wrong, the risk of discovering what one doesn't know or understand, even the risk of sacrifice and loss. But that risk is also what pays the best dividends; it teaches humility, deepens conviction, increases love, and broadens one's sense of the world. Moreover, the experiences of young Latter-day Saints living for an extended period across the world in order to share the gospel brings great benefits to the people they teach as well as to the church. It's a paradox that the deeper one's convictions are about what matters most, the greater one's awareness of how much more there is to know and understand about the world. That awareness leads to increased tolerance that not only requires us to respect each other but also inspires us to protect the right of others to express and share their religious views.

In everything I do as a Christian and in every relationship, I believe I am morally obligated to try to heal, to bring joy, and to do good. This is what amounts to bringing others to Christ, to whatever extent they are willing or interested. Sometimes that involves sharing openly the message of Christianity, and sometimes it involves simply serving others with consistency and integrity and genuine love without any mention of God or Christ; but in all cases it shouldn't be surprising that Christians are striving to consecrate the whole of their lives for the sake of all others—in every relationship and in every circumstance. I enjoyed missionary work so much that had my church provided a professional path to being clergy, I would have taken it. I could have happily done such work for the rest of my life. But I began to have aching concerns the gospel would change lives more profoundly and more sustainably if people were also empowered with greater understanding of the world and of themselves through education. I wanted more of that for myself too. This is why I am a teacher in the humanities but also why I remain active as a lay member of my church, serving whenever and however I can. I am grateful that full-time missionary service and full-time dedication to sacred learning can be part of a larger life plan that includes secular service and secular learning.

There will be many loved ones who will not understand or who will lose respect for a young man or woman who decides to serve a mission. I was fortunate that I did not encounter too much of that. My family was especially supportive, although I suppose some of my friends might have cooled off without telling me their reasons. I cannot say enough about how remarkable it is to see as many young people as I do at Brigham Young University make this decision. And I cannot give proper account of the hundreds of testimonies I have heard over the years after their return, the vast majority of whom feel they too would jump at the chance to go again. And I believe with all my heart that there is no other way at such a young age that I could have gained so many opportunities to learn about and love such a remarkably broad range of people. The greatest joy of taking the risk of being a missionary is the discovery of one's capacity for love. As President Gordon B. Hinckley once said to investigators of the church, "Bring with you all that you have of good and truth . . . and let us see if we may add to it."[1] As a missionary, I was not taught to judge unrighteously or condemn or to

---

1. Gordon B. Hinckley, "The Marvelous Foundation of Our Faith," *Ensign*, November 2002, 81.

manipulate or intellectually convince others. I *was* taught to try to empower others to receive their own revelations. I was occasionally overzealous and judged others when I shouldn't have, but the overall arc of what I experienced taught me patient and enduring appreciation for a wider variety of people than I had ever before imagined.

No one was more changed by my service as a missionary than I was. It would be one thing to stand on the shores of a newly discovered island, like Columbus of old, and blithely declare the land to be the property of a Christian sovereign, without venturing one step farther inland, without learning a word of the language or a single chapter of the history of the people who live there, without venturing any risk to one's own sense of the world. I wish people today could appreciate what it means for young people to walk in the streets among all kinds of people, to eat and talk and live as they do in humility and simplicity and to learn life on their terms, to speak to them in their homes, and to work to earn their trust not because the missionaries have something to gain from them but because they only hope for the people's deeper happiness.

My missionary service has been the foundation of everything I have done ever since. I continue to draw strength from those experiences, and it makes me happy and hopeful and grateful to remember them. About a decade after my mission, I found myself stuck in a mild depression. I reread my missionary journals slowly and deliberately over a few months, and I was a different and happier person when I finished—more hopeful, prayerful, and believing. I would say now that I am less motivated to persuade others to believe as I do and more worried, quite simply, that I will die without having duly honored what I have witnessed. That's a subtle but important difference in motivation. There is an inherent reward in learning how to honor one's sacred experiences, and one of the best ways, I have learned, is to share.

TEMPLE WORK

When I was in my last year of graduate school at Berkeley, I was given the opportunity to teach a class I had designed on the various meanings of genealogy in American literature. I was intent on showing how important genealogy was to the formation of identity in American experience and yet how antithetical and even oppositional American experience can be to the task of preserving genealogical memory. The American dream posits that it doesn't matter where one comes from and that everyone can "make it." While this is a beautiful tribute to the equality and potential of all human beings, it can also slip into a narrative that implies that the past is something to be ignored and discarded and that our dependence on what and who have come before us is a weakness. As part of the class assignment, I required the students to write a family history that recounted, at least as far back as their grandparents, what they could learn of their own family story. This kind of exercise is not unusual for most Latter-day Saints, but it was surprising to me how unusual it was for many of those students. On the whole, their genealogical memory had indeed been pretty shallow, but it was also clear that the experience itself was a valuable exercise in self-discovery. It also gave me an extraordinary snapshot of the diversity of American experience as I read Middle Eastern, Asian, Native American, African American, Irish American, and many other stories.

Latter-day Saint temples are the reason why Latter-day Saints care about genealogy. And this is because the temple represents the site where generations of families, even the entirety of the human family, are joined together into eternity by the sealing power of the priesthood. The reason the temple is a cornerstone of why I am a Latter-day Saint is simple. If a religion believes in its own universality and in the idea of its own saving power but cannot provide adequate means of providing those teachings and saving ordinances to the whole human family, it strikes me that religion becomes just a method for condemning the majority of the human family. I am not sure I could accept the premises of Christianity without the temple. Why believe in a religion that condemns so many people just for lacking adequate oppor-

> Religion cannot obtain its greatest force in the world if it is motivated by nothing more than a "live and let live" philosophy. Religion is a call for changing the world, and so it must lead its adherents to some kind of urgency about effectuating that change.

tunities for understanding and accepting truth, especially when such circumstances can hardly be claimed to be their fault? Some lack opportunities because of extreme poverty, other accidents of birth and geography, or mental or physical incapacity. Some die entirely too young. Some are blinded by addictions or incapacitated by abuse. The inequality of experience in this mortal life is staggering. It seems that such inequalities should be the very thing a religion redresses and not what it implicitly assumes or creates. I crave some reason to hope for recompense, some retroactive way of shoring up an individual's chance for eternal growth and happiness. It seems to me, then, that a Christian ought to ask, Why the command to be baptized, to accept Christ, when so many have never had the chance?

As I see it, globally speaking, all religions are minorities. And religions generally haven't thought through very well how their universal ideas fit within the matrix of a complex and diverse human history, and the obvious blunders this has caused have led some to conclude that we might as well throw out hope in universal truth. For some people, it might be tempting to leave their faith because the truth claims seem too narrow and because they find themselves admiring the truths found in other traditions. But then they likely discover that any religion, once they get down in the weeds, so to speak, of its practices and community, is only narrowly understood and practiced by most adherents. They end up with the same dilemma they started with in their own traditions: how can I espouse beliefs that are universal while still remaining tolerant, patient, and appreciative of the truths espoused by others? How can I espouse beliefs and testify of their veracity while also acknowledging that the truth of God is always greater than our understanding of him?

All religions must make some sense of their truths in light of the fact that the world is so diverse. If the only answer is that we must seek to convert as many people as possible, as quickly as possible, then it seems to me that we end up with the problems of zealous intolerance that have plagued Christianity throughout its history. Baptism becomes so desperately important that the ends sometimes are used to justify the means and Christians bypass the need for conversion or, worse, resort to violence. A missionary impulse is understandable and even vital, as I have already suggested. Religion cannot obtain its greatest force in the world if it is motivated by nothing more than a "live and let live" philosophy. Religion is a call for changing the world, and so it must lead its adherents to some kind of urgency about effectuating that change or, as was wisely said by Mahatma Gandhi, at least become the change we wish to see in the world. That seems to be the energy behind personal repentance and the integrity to then share the grounds for one's own peace and happiness with others.

But the fact is, the world is obstinately resistant to any monopoly on it to which any particular religion might wish to lay claim. And so religiously motivated urgency must be tempered by religiously motivated patience. But where might that patience come from? For me it comes from temples. The zeal of a missionary is balanced by the patience of a temple worker. In the restored gospel, temples are founded on the idea that this life, though essential as a testing ground for our decisions and vital to our opportunities in the next life, is not the only opportunity for growth and change. Temples exist because in Latter-day Saint belief learning, growing, serving, and repenting continue after this life is over—so much so, in fact, that those born and raised without even the remotest chance for understanding the truth of God's ways can still come to understanding and still receive God's blessings as if they had been born right in the heart of God's covenants. This does seem to give us pause, then, in believing that all depends on missionary work alone. It doesn't. The call of the living is also to serve and assist the dead by providing them with the opportunity to receive the saving ordinances of the gospel of Jesus Christ and to have the fullest opportunity to flourish in the next life. The temple also suggests that the call of the dead is to assist the living. They are among us, not leaving us alone in the tasks of life but actively seeking our welfare.

In the Latter-day Saint understanding, the ordinances performed in the temple on behalf of the dead still respect free will. A living person performs an ordinance, such as baptism, on behalf of someone, often an ancestor, who has passed away, and that ancestor has the free will to choose or reject the ordinance, just as we enjoy those same freedoms in this life. There is nothing binding about such an exercise at this point, but it is an expression of love and appreciation for one's heritage and for strangers and a profound expression of hope in the universality of the human family and of the redeeming powers of the atonement of Jesus Christ. And it is based in the hope that such ordinances, if accepted by the deceased, will become efficacious by unlocking the full potential of any individual soul to continue to progress after this life.

What happens inside the temple is as edifying and instructive for the dead as it is for the living. This is not the result of some strange occult practice but rather the result of the opportunity to revisit the very purpose of the world's creation, which is to bless the entirety of the human family, and to revisit our role in life before we came here, in life here on earth, and in life forever after. In the temple one gains greater commitment to live closer to God's commandments, greater respect for God's creations, and a deeper appreciation for one's inheritance. Temples were one of the most important fruits of Joseph Smith's extraordinary vision of how the gospel of Jesus Christ might benefit every living soul equally. His was a vision of being able to bring every child of God within proximity of His face by inviting a deeper sanctification of one's life in the temple, the very house of the Lord.

It is customary in the church for people to go through the temple to receive what are called their endowments shortly before a mission or marriage. In my case I was months away from leaving on my mission to Venezuela, and I attended the temple for the first time. I felt cautiously excited about what I was experiencing. It was new and somewhat unfamiliar to me. I hadn't been raised with a lot of teaching about the temple, so it took some time to adjust. And just as I was preparing to go on my mission, I realized that my brother, who had died of suicide just a little over a year earlier, had not been able to receive the Melchizedek Priesthood, which is customarily given to a young man as he enters adulthood, and that I could therefore go through the temple for him, on his behalf. I had received what is known as my patriarchal blessing, and in it I was told that there were still things I could do to be of service to my brother. I hadn't understood how or what that could be, but now I did. What a great blessing it was to feel that his story was not over, that he had not written the final chapter of his life, and that I might play some role in helping that process continue. I had already come to know that he was at peace. I knew his suffering had been relieved, but relief of suffering is not an end in itself but an opportunity for growth and learning. My brother had always been fascinated by great minds, by great ideas, by beautiful music, and by scientific discoveries, and those who knew and loved him knew that a great mind had been cut short of its opportunity to contribute to the world. I was eager to give him the chance to expand his knowledge and understanding.

I went through the temple for him just weeks before departing on my mission, and not long afterward I received a very personal and very clear revelation in the form of a dream that my brother was progressing and growing beyond my ability to fully understand and that he was grateful for what I had done. As I indicated earlier, personal revelations of this kind provide the bedrock of my faith. I have often felt his presence near me and my family.

The temple is the great promise of eternal progress, of second and third and fourth chances, however many it takes. It provides the circumstances and the means by which life's many injustices might find more balance and mercy. It provides the means to hold families together even when in this life, for reasons we don't always understand, people take different paths. I believe that the promises of the temple extend to the entirety of the human family, and this brings me great patience in the face of opposition and struggle and wide and sometimes dizzying diversity across the world. It tells me that no one person's story is finished at the end of life and that we all belong, sealed and adopted into the great promises first given to Abraham. It tells me that this life is just a brief, albeit important, moment in our overall development.

Isaiah uses a phrase that has always fascinated me. He tells us to rejoice, "for more are the children of the desolate than the children of the married wife. . . . Enlarge the place of thy tent" (Isaiah 54:1–2). Indeed, genealogy teaches us how dependent our unique individuality is on a myriad of people across time and space and therefore how much broader and inclusive our sense of belonging needs to be if we are going to be agents in bringing the human family together. No family line is perfectly straight or singular, no family story is without disruption, disappointment, and heartache, or without brokenness and loss, and no family line is independent of all others. All family lines extend not only back in time but across cultures and geographies, teaching us our relation to and dependency on everyone else and helping us understand that to find ourselves reunited with each other and with God requires the rule of adoption and not birthrights, patience and not intolerance, forbearance and not swift judgment.

On Criticism, Compassion, and Charity

I am deeply humbled by this invitation to share my journey as a scholar of faith. I have wrestled with my feelings these past few weeks because I am not sure how much of my experience is applicable to others, nor am I entirely sure that I have enough answers. I do know that I want to communicate honestly, and, most importantly, I want to edify and strengthen your faith. The challenge is that my journey is idiosyncratic. However, I take comfort in two things. Although your stories are different from mine, yours are just as idiosyncratic. There are as many ways of reaching Christ as there are people in this world. As Elder Bruce C. Hafen has said, "Nothing brings the Spirit into a conversation or a classroom more than hearing people bear honest testimony, not so much by exhortation as by just telling the story

This chapter is a lightly edited version of a lecture delivered on November 11, 2015, at Brigham Young University as part of the "My Journey as a Scholar of Faith" series sponsored by the BYU Faculty Center. The original speech was later published in *BYU Studies Quarterly* 55, no. 3 (2016).

of their personal experience."[1] So I seek to speak candidly, but also in love and respect for the dignity of every person here.

This is part autobiography and testimony, but it is also an argument. And here's my thesis: I believe that the humanities

---

Criticism, compassion, and charity often work together but sometimes get separated, and when they do, the quality of our intellectual and spiritual lives suffers.

---

are not just an adornment but are essential to our spiritual lives, and by that I also mean that intellectual and spiritual growth need to occur in at least some relation to one another. However, neither religion nor the humanities can have the greatest impact and best influence in our lives without three crucial ingredients: criticism, compassion, and charity. These three things often work together but sometimes get separated, and when they do, the quality of our intellectual and spiritual lives suffers.

Let me start by explaining that criticism is not the same thing as contention. Contention isn't what happens when people disagree. It is what happens when they lose trust and respect for one another. Criticism, on the other hand, is the means by which we protect ourselves from deception and by which we strengthen our autonomy as moral agents. It implies that we can

---

1.   Bruce C. Hafen, *A Disciple's Life: The Biography of Neal A. Maxwell* (Salt Lake City: Deseret Book, 2010), xiv.

see ourselves in a context of difference and plurality. In critical thinking we distance ourselves from an experience or from some idea enough to assess and judge its value and interpret its meaning. Without criticism, we are swept up by the whims of opinion; we parrot what we read or watch or listen to.

Compassion is an important companion to criticism. If we never allow ourselves to feel what others feel or to see through another's eyes, our critical judgment will become centripetal and self-reinforcing. We will end up talking only to those we already like or identify with. It can lead to cynicism and categorical mistrust of others. Compassion, which means to "suffer with," can trigger learning and change. And as our own baptismal covenant implies, it is what we owe everyone, both those most different and those most familiar. It helps us not to overgeneralize or bypass the particular circumstances of individuals. Of course, compassion without criticism runs centrifugal risks, something akin to gullibility, in which we feel impressions, attractions, and distractions at every turn.

Charity, I want to suggest, is the means by which we learn to live with the tension between criticism and compassion. And I want to make it clear that wherever charity emerges, there Christ is also. We know its characteristics: long-suffering, believing, trusting, not easily offended. As the Mexican poet Octavio Paz says, charity is akin to what a metaphor does: it holds differences together in a meaningful relationship without collapsing those differences.[2] Charity helps us not to be driven by emotion, to weigh things in the balance, both the good and the difficult, and it recognizes there is a gap between our thoughts and God's thoughts that we must seek to overcome by a perpetual search for more truth. In this way charity helps us avoid polarized and

---

2.   Octavio Paz, *The Other Voice: Essays on Modern Poetry* (New York: Mariner Books, 1992), 158.

polarizing conclusions. This is why a personal commitment to repentance and humility and a steady practice of submission to God's will and a constant plea for Christ's pure love are essential to thinking clearly.

The humanities are a wonderful training ground for charity. They teach us how to imagine communion. They are methods for experiencing reconciliation, for imagining beauty and meaning in the wake of chaos and suffering, and for connecting us to one another and to the cosmos. Reading great literature, learning languages, listening to music, watching live theater or great films, participating in religious ritual—these are all experiences aimed at reinvigorating and expanding our sense of self and belonging in the world. Nothing captures the way literature can teach charity more beautifully than this statement by C. S. Lewis: "Literary experience heals the wound, without undermining the privilege, of individuality. . . . In reading great literature I become a thousand men and yet remain myself. . . . Here, as in worship, in love, in moral action, and in knowing, I transcend myself; and am never more myself than when I do."[3] Without the experience of charity, we are prone to the allures of mass emotions that obliterate particularity, or perhaps worse, we face what some have called balkanization—the abandonment of the quest for community and the retreat to our own like-minded camps.

Sometimes I have experienced charity in the arts and sometimes in religious contexts. I don't think God is as interested in the distinctions we like to make between the sacred and the secular. For example, a few years ago my son Sam and I flew out to Los Angeles to visit my brother. As we sat listening to Mahler's Second Symphony performed by the Los Angeles Symphony, we all wept at the words "What was created / Must perish, / What

---

3. C. S. Lewis, *An Experiment in Criticism* (Cambridge: Cambridge University Press, 1961), 140–41.

perished, rise again! / Cease from trembling! / Prepare yourself to live!" I was both transported and grounded, purely loved and invited to change. Then there was the time when, on a research trip to Chile, I sat in the celestial room in the Santiago Chile Temple by myself at a particular desperate and low point for me. I imagined what it would be like to have my deceased brother by my side, and suddenly I felt the real presence of his arms wrapped around me. I felt guided in my research from that moment. On another occasion, I was called to serve in a stake presidency and Elder Marcus Nash asked me in an interview to imagine what I would say if Jesus were in the room alone with me. At that moment Christ's presence became unmistakably real, and I was overcome with tears and could only mumble "Thank you." I felt forgiven, accepted, known, and loved. And called to serve. It was empowering to discover how much I loved Christ.

I have also had this experience when listening to church leaders, which gave me a foundational witness of their calling as his special witnesses. I can still recall as a missionary in the MTC the way my hair felt blown back (short as it was) by sheer force of testimony of the living Christ from Elders Dallin H. Oaks and Neal A. Maxwell—and similarly from Elder Henry B. Eyring when he was a Seventy visiting my stake in Oakland when I was in graduate school, from Elder D. Todd Christofferson when he was a Seventy visiting my stake in Flagstaff when I taught there before coming to BYU, and twice from Elder M. Russell Ballard here in Provo. In each case I have felt the unmistakable presence of the Savior and experienced and received their witness of his living reality. These experiences have anchored my hope and faith in the restored gospel. In each case God's love healed me of doubt, hurt, pain, and discouragement. Doubts sometimes benefit from answers, but most often doubt springs from fear, anxiety, abandonment, or lack of self-confidence. For this reason doubt is best resolved not with knowledge per se, but in loving relationships and with experiences of God's pure love. Nothing is more important to experience than this.

What I want to suggest is that aesthetic and spiritual experiences teach that understanding matters and it comes, but it doesn't matter most and it doesn't come first. As the great Spanish poet Miguel de Unamuno says in his inimitable masterpiece, *The Tragic Sense of Life*, "The primary reality is not that I think, but that I live." Thus, "the end purpose of life is to live, not to understand."[4] In other words, truth is to be lived more than it is to be apprehended. The most painful and challenging times are invariably the most transformative, even and especially when we don't understand. If we refuse to absorb contradiction and instead rush to premature or shallow explanations, we may end up shielding ourselves from Christ's experience of the matter. The same principle applies to marriage. My wife Amy and I might not always love each other as we should, and we don't always understand or agree with each other. But as we strive for unity and loyalty in the face of those differences, not despite them, our experience deepens and our character changes.

My first experiences with criticism, compassion, and charity were in family life at home. As Latter-day Saints, we lived as a very small minority outside New York. We were taught to love human diversity and that God must too. Dinner table conversation at my home was free-flowing, covering politics and culture and the church. We went to concerts and museums in the city and we hosted friends of other faiths at our home. I was the youngest of three brothers, and the older two were exceptionally bright and observant and full of strong opinions. They read serious literature at young ages, they loved and played classical music, and they knew how to have a meaningful experience in a

---

4. Miguel de Unamuno, *The Tragic Sense of Life* (Princeton: Princeton University Press, 1972), 41, 129.

museum. Even though neither of my parents would have considered themselves experts, they remain among my most important adjudicators of taste. They have always been amateurs in the best sense of the word: lovers of all good things, consistent with the charitable work, as Mormon describes it, of "lay[ing] hold upon every good thing" (Moroni 7:25).

I enjoyed the conversations, but I was intimidated a bit at first. I didn't feel that I had a good vocabulary, and I couldn't express myself well, and when I looked at a painting or listened to a symphony, I wasn't sure what I was supposed to feel. I preferred sports, rock and roll, and goofing off. And honestly, I was really, really good at that. My goofing off was innocent at first, but it led me into a struggle with keeping the Word of Wisdom

---

My parents were adamant that I not become selfishly attracted only to like-minded or similar personalities but that I branch out.

---

and prolonged spiritual doubts. The good thing was that my parents never seemed overly impatient with me, even though my brothers were much further advanced in their critical skills and life skills. My parents thought going to church was generally a good idea but not the most important thing. In fact, when we asked our dad why he occasionally decided to stay home or go home early from church, he explained, with a wry grin, that once you went to church three thousand times, it was optional. What mattered most to my parents was being a good person. The most painful conversations I ever had with them pertained to situations in which I was struggling to be inclusive or kind to difficult personalities. They were adamant that I not become selfishly attracted only to like-minded or similar personalities but that I branch out. I watched my parents reach out to extended family, many of whom grew up in economic and cultural circumstances far less privileged than my own. I admired how they could talk to the very poor and the very rich without changing their tone. I am especially grateful for the fact that whenever the conversation got too critical of people or leaders, my parents always helped each other and us to remember to be charitable.

I suppose that according to some litmus tests they weren't exactly the most active or model Latter-day Saints, but anyone who knows them, knows them to be profoundly Christian. They didn't follow all the rules exactly, nor did they seem particularly worried that I did so. I never remember my parents getting on my case about grades, about Scout advancement, or about going on a mission. I think they trusted me and trusted that their example of good living would pull us through. They were right. They were loath to reduce the pursuit of a good life to a rat race or a checklist. My mother often expressed frustration that the formal practices of religion just didn't seem to work for her as it did for others. My father was never entirely satisfied by answers he was given to his questions, but my parents never allowed anger or hatred or despair to rule their own hearts or to govern their approach to life. They had better things to do and to see and to understand in the world. They aren't perfect, but I wish more people were like them.

Maybe they didn't feel they could be the ones to plant the seed of the restored gospel in its entirety, but they were careful not to trample the soil of my faith with their own overstated doubts. As we have been taught by Elder Jeffrey R. Holland and President Dieter F. Uchtdorf, doubting our doubts can be an expression of faith.[5] Without my parents' forbearance, I don't believe I would have had the freedom to discover my own testimony of the restored gospel. Criticism or disagreement is not an enemy to faith and belief. What seems to undermine faith and belief is distrust and fear directed at ourselves, others, or God, and it can lead, paradoxically, to inflexible and dogmatic thinking.

Elder Maxwell warned us not to "oversponsor" our ideas. Instead, he said, "let the Spirit impel our worthy ideas," by which I think he means we should be careful not to assume we have arrived at the proper conclusions about reality.[6] Thinking is an experiment, not a test. Sometimes I am embarrassed for football players who celebrate a sack on second down only to be burned by a touchdown pass on the next play. I have learned that on the most sensitive and the most divisive issues, instead of tightening up and prematurely interpreting the meaning of a situation, we should be more careful to listen to all sides. Such listening puts us in the position to do our most creative and best thinking. Derek Walcott insists, for example, that great poetry can never be based in revenge, anger, or nostalgia but only in acceptance and assimilation of the facts of experience.[7] If we truly wish to "enlarge the place of [our] tent" (Isaiah 54:2), we must not chase people off by shaming them for their questions. They need a refuge, as they are, while they wait upon the Lord.

Many years ago during a job interview at an eastern university, I was faced with a roomful of scholars. During the question-and-answer session, someone asked my opinion about a

---

5. Jeffrey R. Holland, "Lord, I Believe," *Ensign*, May 2013, 94; Dieter F. Uchtdorf, "Come, Join with Us," *Ensign*, November 2013, 23.
6. Neal A. Maxwell, "'Repent of [Our] Selfishness' (D&C 56:8)," *Ensign*, May 1999, 23.
7. Derek Walcott, "The Muse of History," in *What the Twilight Says: Essays* (New York: Farrar, Straus and Giroux, 1998), 36–64.

book related to my research. I hadn't even heard of the book, so I couldn't even give a half-baked answer. I just said in front of everyone, "I don't know the book, so I can't answer the question." Afterward, a member of the search committee expressed admiration that I had the courage to say, "I don't know." He said, "I wish more of us had that kind of courage." That may have been the only time in my academic life when ignorance was a virtue, not enough of a virtue to get me the job, mind you, but it was nice for once to be congratulated for being ignorant.

In his marvelous essay "The Way of Ignorance," Wendell Berry insists that the burden of the Gospels is to "accept our failure to understand, not as a misstatement or a textual flaw or as a problem to be solved, but as a question to live with and a burden to be borne."[8] We might know some things. We might even be in possession of some fundamental truths, but truth is no trophy you can hold up. Its value isn't in possessing it. Its value is the love we muster to build relationships in its pursuit. This is why we need God, each other, even our enemies, to teach us truth. Paul made it clear: you can talk truth all the day long, but if you don't have charity, you have nothing (1 Corinthians 13:1–3). There is something truer than truth, and it is love.

So my parents didn't pass on knowledge to me so much as they allowed my experiences to be deep, authentic, and my own. They insisted I do with my life what I most wanted. They told me to go to the school of my choosing and to major in a field that appealed to me. This is particularly marvelous when you consider their burdens. They were in the midst of striving to help their firstborn, Kenny, through terrible depression that eventually led to his suicide; helping their second son, Bill, deal with the intensity of coming to terms with his homosexuality; and

---

8.   Wendell Berry, *The Way of Ignorance and Other Essays* (Washington, DC: Shoemaker and Hoard, 2005), 131.

helping me, their youngest, to emergence from the fog of a misspent adolescence. They never pointed fingers at each other after the death of their son, and they worked through the process of Bill's coming out with grace and care, managing to keep their own marriage strong, their relationship to both their sons locked in even as we took different paths, and their relationship to people of all persuasions and to the church open and fair. Crucially, they taught my brother and me to love each other. Their example of thoughtful criticism, compassion, and charity is perhaps the most heroic and most Christian example I have in my life, even though it isn't tied formally to institutional life in the restored church. I love the church. It is where I belong. It is where we all belong, to my mind, but I have never hesitated to love and admire my parents or anyone else who does good work in the world outside the walls of my church. I believe Christ would expect nothing less from me.

I wouldn't have gone to Stanford, majored in comparative literature, or taken my career path as a professor without my brother Bill's example, encouragement, and brilliance that lighted every step of the way for me through my education. He was and is my intellectual soul mate. My freshman year at Stanford included a yearlong, dorm-based intensive course on the Western tradition, perhaps the single most valuable educational experience of my life. In the hallways and in class, we debated the meaning of Greek tragedies, the value of biblical wisdom, and the very nature of the universe. We wrestled with Darwinism, the meaning of grace according to Luther, the root causes of poverty, and the legacies of the Holocaust. I was debating with atheists, with other Christians, with Muslims and Jews and Hindus. This, for me, was heaven! The experience that year was enough to convince me I wanted to make a career out of reading, discussing, and writing about great ideas. What was especially exciting was that we could explore ideas without restraint, without preestablished conclusions, and in the company of a wide diversity of viewpoints. I learned that part of criticism is listening to the criticism of others, something central to scholarly work. I felt comfortable saying something that I might later decide was utter hogwash. I was often told my ideas were, indeed, hogwash, although my friends used other words for it. Sometimes it meant I got stinging and hurtful criticisms of my beliefs, but more often than not such exchanges helped me recognize my own sexism or racism or naivete about the world. I sensed that one of my professors—an atheist, a Jew, and a Marxist—was not thrilled with the idea of my wanting to serve a mission, but he also had a respect and interest in the restored gospel. He had already read the Book of Mormon but wanted to read more, so I gave him a collection of essays by one of my most influential models of a Latter-day Saint scholar in those days, Gene England, which he enjoyed. When I got too worked up in my criticism of a writer, whether it was Marx or Nietzsche, he would ask me if I was reading carefully enough to understand that author's point of view. I figured that if he had bothered to read about my faith, I should bother to be as curious about other ideas.

I was fortunate to have spent my summer before and after my freshman year with another pivotal model for me, Lowell Bennion. I worked as a counselor at his boys' ranch. Lowell was a man who balanced criticism, compassion, and charity better than anyone I knew. I also devoured his books in those days, as I did the books of another important influence, Elder Maxwell. Both were men of learning and of careful and bold judgment, but they also devoted their lives not to thinking brilliantly, as brilliant as they were, but to service. Lowell took time to treat my wounds in the wake of my brother's tragic death, and he helped me keep things simple when looking at the church and thinking about the gospel. He had lived with his questions, particularly about blacks and the priesthood, and he never stopped asking them openly and honestly, but he also never let such questions overshadow his life or lead him to anger. For him, life always boiled down to "What can I do to help?" What a gift that man was.

My one semester at BYU after my freshman year and before my mission exposed me to many more professors and peers who modeled lives of integrity, intellectual curiosity, and deep faith. It was an embarrassment of riches. Indeed, Brigham Young's vision of education sunk deep into my soul and ultimately drew me back to BYU to teach. As I think about it now, it was as if I always knew I would be there. Since my arrival there almost eighteen years ago, I have taught, recreated, researched, worshipped, mourned, and rejoiced with my exceptional peers, women and men who are among the most remarkable people I have ever known. Our conversations together on complex and difficult topics have been the most exciting and soul-fulfilling conversations in my life. And I cannot overstate how much I admire and love the students at BYU. I will always defend this place and believe in it as the most exciting and important experiment in higher education. We don't always get things right at BYU, of course. We sometimes prefer to coerce consensus or to micromanage it. We are overly anxious about differences of opinion. I think it probably comes with the territory of engaging in an unusual but essential experiment. Elder Holland says, "In this Church there is an enormous amount of room, and scriptural commandment, for studying and learning, for comparing and considering, for discussion and awaiting further revelation. . . . In this there is no place for coercion or manipulation, no place for intimidation or hypocrisy."[9] I hope we can work harder to create an atmosphere for honest conversation and exploration as brothers and sisters. Since faith is strengthened more by relationships than by ideas, this is vital.

---

9.   Jeffrey R. Holland, "A Prayer for the Children," *Ensign*, May 2003, 85.

We can do better than what at Stanford and at Berkeley was a conversation limited to a hermeneutics of suspicion, that is, a method of interpretation that starts and ends at a position of distrust. Don't get me wrong. I believe in the worth of such suspicion. I believe it can keep at bay a whole host of evils. I believe it has helped me, for example, to keep my distance from the allures of capitalism, from the seductions of propagandistic punditry, from the sometimes false illusions of our own national innocence, and from the glossy appearances of a mythologized past. I think it was useful for understanding the kind of persecution we suffered as Latter-day Saints, which I think is why I found myself drawn to minority discourse in graduate school. I was suspicious of the ways in which majority cultures and hegemonic discourses forge and perpetuate their own authority by means of denigrating, ignoring, or otherwise oppressing minority voices. This is perhaps why I became a comparatist. It helped me check the norms and assumptions of one culture against those of another.

But a hermeneutics of suspicion can lead to a categorical suspicion of the centers of power and of all kinds of authority. It can motivate us to be more cynical, less trusting, and angrier than everyone else. As Alan Jacobs brilliantly described, it is an attitude of distrust that "would rather suffer anything than the humiliation of being fooled."[10] Ultimately this leaves us feeling utterly and totally self-satisfied with ourselves and our own like-minded crowd. After listening to a particularly tiresome rant against Republicans by my colleagues one day at Berkeley, I remember asking if any of them actually had any Republican friends. I was met with blank stares. Liberals don't have a corner on paranoia and mistrust of everyone else, however. During my one semester at BYU in the fall of 1984, I once said to my friend

---

10. Alan Jacobs, *A Theology of Reading: The Hermeneutics of Love* (Boulder, CO: Westview Press, 2001), 88.

as we crossed campus, "Sometimes it feels around here as if people believe a good Mormon can't be a Democrat." Just as I said this, a student passing us turned and yelled, "You *can't* be a good Mormon and a Democrat!" I guess apparently you can't have a majority of like-minded people without your share of chauvinists either. Suspicion today is the ethos of government, the ethos of public discourse, and the ethos of civic duty.

I prefer what scholars have called a hermeneutics of love, or of recovery, a way of interpreting that uses criticism to complete

---

The most appropriate response to limited human instruments through whom inspiration comes is not deconstructive cynicism or condemnation but the creativity to help build on the portion of inspiration offered.

---

or fulfill or restore. It is the difference between looking for the faults of others in order to justify mistrust or using those faults as a way to measure how the Spirit nevertheless moves through weak human vessels. To my mind, it is Christian to see what it is an author or artist aspired to, even if she didn't quite achieve it. This is what I learned from Caribbean novelist and theorist Edouard Glissant, who admired the white Southern writer William Faulkner but also suspected that his representations of black characters and women were perhaps a symptom of his own biases. Faulkner's racism mattered, but Glissant decided it was better to imagine and work to complete the vision of a post-slavery world of which Faulkner was first to catch an essential glimpse.[11] In other words, the most appropriate response to limited human instruments through whom inspiration comes is not deconstructive cynicism or condemnation but the creativity to help build on the portion of inspiration offered. Similarly, when I was ordained as a bishop, the stake president told me to listen for what his blessing was trying to say. I thought that was good advice for any Sunday.

The other day two young friends from my ward asked me how I reconcile a belief in the universal claims of the restored gospel with the diversity of the world. What a great and important question! I suppose I would say that the challenge of doing so is itself so much more meaningful than giving up on the possibility of truth. Give up on the idea of a universal truth and there is no challenge left, since you end up abdicating the responsibility to discern. We have to believe in something, even if it is only an absolute belief in absolute relativism. The benefit of a belief in God is that by making you answerable for your sins, it helps you avoid creating a worldview made after your own whims and appetites. Once you begin to trust in the living God, you begin to experience his love, which as Nephi teaches is enough to keep you on the good path even with unanswered questions (see 1 Nephi 11:17).

As I started college, I knew at least the meaning of God's love. When my oldest brother took his life in the middle of my senior year after a prolonged battle with clinical depression, I was comforted one night when I experienced the living presence of my brother in my bedroom and received confirmation that he was at peace and that he loved us. I knew then that God was

---

11. Edouard Glissant, *Faulkner, Mississippi*, trans. Barbara Lewis and Thomas C. Spear (New York: Farrar, Straus, and Giroux, 1988).

involved in the details of my life, not to the degree, of course, that he will always arrange things to my liking or prevent terrible things from happening, but that he will respond to our experiences with genuine compassion and mercy. I still want to know why biology seemed to have betrayed my brother. I still want to know why anyone should have to suffer severe mental illness. But God's love took me one step further. As mentioned earlier, my patriarchal blessing told me there were things I could still do for my brother. After I performed the temple ordinances for him, I had a dream in which he told me with great excitement that he was learning so much from the best teachers. You had to know his insatiable curiosity for learning to appreciate what that meant. I knew then that the ordinances of the temple were effectual for life after death, that the powers of the atonement reached beyond the grave, and that my brother was progressing beyond his earthly limitations.

On my mission a few years later, I read in the writings of Joseph Fielding Smith that he felt a member of the church should never go through the temple for someone who had committed suicide.[12] This was disappointing, to be sure, but I didn't bristle at this nor feel inclined to judge. I have never said anything about it publicly until now. I don't recall that I said anything to anyone about it. I want to be clear: I don't share this to undermine trust in the leaders of the church. I say it because maybe it is helpful to someone who might be struggling to realize that such contradictions shouldn't cancel out your knowledge of God's love. The general consensus of the General Authorities over time on the essentials of the gospel is what matters most. Styles, personalities, isolated statements, and even policies can change, but the fundamentals of the gospel—obedience, service, repentance,

---

12. Joseph Fielding Smith, *Doctrines of Salvation* (Salt Lake City: Bookcraft, 1992), 2:338.

and faith—do not. Our challenge and responsibility is to hold fast to the iron rod, especially in the mists of darkness when we can't see clearly. Keeping ourselves committed to the fundamentals will not always provide answers to our questions, but it will provide the strength to live with the questions. If that consensus still conflicts with our beliefs, we can be like Lowell Bennion: still look for and uphold the good and truth of the church, keep our covenants, love and serve generously, keep asking questions,

> Keeping ourselves committed to the fundamentals will not always provide answers to our questions, but it will provide the strength to live with the questions.

and wait on the Lord. The important thing is to maintain access to Christ's healing power and keep ourselves open to the possibility of more understanding.

Criticism and compassion can sometimes create sparks of tension. Church life is a source of great joy, but it can also be a source of sorrow. I am fiercely loyal to the church, but I struggle to agree with everything that is said or done by church leaders. I admire so many in the church who stay and thrive, and I miss and long for so many good people who have gone, people I fear we didn't make enough room for. I love my temple marriage to Amy and all that it has given us, but I also deeply love and feel great compassion for my one and only remaining sibling,

Bill. Given what happened to our oldest brother, perhaps others can understand the anxiety it causes me to know that I might be the cause of any more pain. The policy change in November 2015 regarding gay couples was an acutely hard challenge in this regard. I love the leaders of this church. I trust them. I know they pray and act on behalf of all God's children. It is important to remember, as a believing gay friend of mine says, that there are no bad guys here. It is certainly true that my difficulty is because I am not valiant enough. But I believe that in my sorrows and my contradictory feelings, I share something of the contradiction it was for Jesus to feel abandoned by his Father and friends just at the moment when he fulfilled his Father's will and suffered everything for all of us. Christ suffered even this moment, you see. Because of his charity, no one's feelings are unknown to him; no one's perspective is incapable of finding a basis in an important truth. If you feel tempted to leave, please reconsider. We need you. We need to hear your pain. We need your questions. We need your gifts. We will all be better for working this through together. It would be, I think, a colossal mistake, not to mention a contradiction, for any of us, no matter our feelings on this issue, to refuse charity for others just because we perceive their actions or views as uncharitable. So look around you. There are others who are hurting. We are all members of the same body. As the humanities teach us, there is something fundamentally healing about listening compassionately to the stories of others. Let's listen together. In this regard, the way the church makes us responsible and answerable to people different than we are is an opportunity to offer our charity widely. I have heard some people say this a "sifting" moment in the church. Let's be clear: you and I have no right to be sifters. We are commanded to be gatherers, one by one.

I still don't understand all things, but I still know that God loves us and that we should love one another. As I have prayed over my family's situation, the Lord has never revealed why things have happened the way they have in my family. Instead he has repeatedly told me, almost to the point of redundancy, to love, love, and love some more. He has told me to relieve the suffering of others. That's it. To have charity. When I have instead focused on wanting answers or on trying to explain or justify things, I find it can make me a bit crazy, and sometimes I get filled with anger. Then there is the temptation of finding someone to blame and feeding an anger addiction. The Internet is good for that. How I wish people of faith would learn to defend their faith with love, not with vitriol. How I wish critics too would exhibit even a modicum of the kind of love they claim the church doesn't have. Even wounds of love can spread hate like toxic pollution if we don't have charity. God is gentle with us, he sorrows with us, and he absorbs the reality of the world day by day with charity and forbearance. Knowing that should give us more reason to be gentle with others.

In answer to my young friends' question, I would say that I have lived long enough to see that the gospel has worked and borne good fruit. When I had finally decided after a few years of Word of Wisdom abuses in high school to keep the commandments, I noticed a remarkable peace come into my life. I felt strong. When I prayed and studied the scriptures, I felt deep longing and connection. All through my challenging and stimulating years at Stanford and at Berkeley, I learned that obedience to the commandments is a low-risk, high-yield proposition and that to deliberately drop God's commandments until my mind could sort everything out was, on the other hand, a high-risk, low-yield proposition. I have sinned and repented often in my life—honestly, I think I am somewhat of an expert. I don't say that to be cute or funny or falsely humble. And it has taught me how easily my mind and worldview shift according to my level of obedience. It has been tempting to change my worldview rather than to change my life. While I am not proud of my mistakes, I will never, ever be ashamed to proclaim the blessings of the atonement of Jesus Christ. Christ has made me what I am and given me everything I have. I am not here because I learned perfect obedience once and for all. I am here only because God is gracious.

One of his most gracious gifts is friends. To tell but one story, I was admitted to Stanford and keen on attending but was worried about having enough support from fellow Latter-day Saints to stay strong. As I prayed about it, I felt I would be all right. At Stanford you fill out a roommate card during the summer, and based on that information, they choose your roommate for you. I didn't indicate my religion since it didn't ask, but I remember writing, "I don't want a roommate who parties too much." My brother helped me move in the first day. My roommate had already moved in, but he wasn't there. On his desk sat a Book of Mormon. My brother and I looked at each other astonished. We thought, was he an anti-Mormon?! This just seemed too improbable. As it turned out, there were only four male Mormons entering the freshman class of fifteen hundred students. My roommate, Andy Sorenson, was from California and also had recently gotten active in the church and decided to go on a mission. He too had arrived at Stanford with a prayer in his heart that he would have help to go on his mission.

God brought us together, and we remain best friends. We helped each other stay active and serve missions, which established a solid foundation for us to later begin our relationships with our respective future wives in that small wonderful Stanford ward. I could have devoted most of my talk to my most important friend, Amy, but suffice it to say that I married a calm, steady, loyal, and brilliant woman whose critical capacities and compassion are exceptional and whose commitment to charity have helped me never take myself or my ideas or my perspective too seriously. She is patient with contradiction, with difficult trials and difficult institutional situations, and has held strong through my darkest hours. She doesn't overreact to my struggles, and she helps me keep things simple. So I guess that moment of grace to start my college career was a small but pivotal and eternally important gift. I started out and remain a free spirit, but I was immature. I was sorrowful too. I could cry easily, and I often did. I could fall apart. I think because of my brother's recent death, I felt at any time that all that I knew and could believe in could be swept up in a dark tornado of violence at any moment. Or that I myself might drop the sacred value of my life on a whim and that would be the end of me. I have lived with a sense of urgency and anxiousness that has kept me clinging to Christ. It's been a life-long struggle, and only the grace of good friends and good family and God's tender mercies have saved me.

Enough experiences with God's love, then, and you will realize something fundamentally good and true about the church and the gospel and also something fundamentally good and true about yourself and your life. Existence itself becomes a miracle and a rare and beautiful gift. This is the basis of my interest and research in environmental stewardship. It isn't because it's a political trend. It's because nature as an expression of Christ's glory has healed me of my sorrows and because creation care is how I show gratitude for his gifts. There is a scene in my favorite novel, Dostoevsky's *The Brothers Karamazov*, that captures how God's love increases our ability to bear contradictions, to withstand doubts, to endure suffering, and to embrace physical life with all our heart. Zosima the monk is Alyosha's spiritual mentor, and he tells Alyosha his entire life story. Zosima says, "Even one day is enough for a man to know all happiness."[13] Think on

---

13. Fyodor Dostoevsky, *The Brothers Karamazov*, trans. Richard Pevear and Larissa Volokhonsky (New York: Farrar, Straus and Giroux, 1990), 289.

that. If we were truly aware of how little we have earned and how much is already given, we would have no needs, no anxieties or dependencies. Going into the monastery, Alyosha was weighed down by unanswered questions about his own life, but he emerges from the monastery and collapses under the weight of life's joy:

> Night, fresh and quiet, almost unstirring, enveloped the earth. The white towers and golden domes of the church gleamed in the sapphire sky. The luxuriant autumn flowers in the flowerbeds near the house had fallen asleep until morning. The silence of the earth seemed to merge with the silence of the heavens, the mystery of

God's pure love is yours for the taking and yours also for the giving, to assist others in their pursuit of deeper happiness in Christ, the Creator and the Redeemer.

> the earth touched the mystery of the stars. . . . Alyosha stood gazing and suddenly, as if he had been cut down, threw himself to the earth. He did not know why he was embracing it, he did not try to understand why he longed so irresistibly to kiss it, to kiss all of it, but he was kissing it, weeping, sobbing, and watering it with his tears, and he vowed ecstatically to love it, to love it unto ages of ages.[14]

---

14. Dostoevsky, *Brothers Karamazov*, 362.

It took me many years to learn to accept myself and to see this exceptional privilege of the bare facts of existence, unadorned by the promises of money or good looks or reputation or fortunate circumstances, and unattached to anxieties about worthiness or being good enough. None of this is earned, you see—this body, this planet, these beautiful people around you, the mountains, the clouds, the very fabric of life's inconceivable diversity. Maybe in some ways that means God's pure love, his charity, can feel impersonal since it is available to anyone. But that's just it. It is universal, so it is yours for the taking and yours also for the giving, to assist others in their pursuit of deeper happiness in Christ, the Creator and the Redeemer. I have, in other words, the privilege and responsibility to love those I come to know in all their individuality and to love my corner of the earth I have come to inhabit in all its particularity. I look around at the bounty of what I have here, and I can do nothing more, and nothing less.

A Poetics of the Restoration

S tarting first with the proposition that the humanities and the Restoration both share an interest in the preservation of threatened knowledge and in the recovery of lost knowledge, I would like to suggest further how these two forms of restoration can enjoin the same labor. Brigham Young dispensed with the notion of a strict distinction between sacred and secular forms of knowledge when he insisted that all truth belongs to the restored gospel of The Church of Jesus Christ of Latter-day Saints, that "every accomplishment, every polished grace, every useful attainment in mathematics, music, and in all sciences and art belong to the Saints."[1] However, this would seem to contradict the notion articulated in the Doctrine and Covenants that the two chief obstacles to our understanding of revealed truth are "disobedience" and "the tradition of [the] fathers" (Doctrine and Covenants 93:39). Or as Paul put it, "Beware lest any man

This is an edited version of an essay that appeared in *BYU Studies* 49, no. 4 (2010): 45–72; reprinted here with permission.

1. Brigham Young, quoted in Spencer W. Kimball, "The Gospel Vision of the Arts," *Ensign*, July 1977, 3.

spoil you through philosophy and vain deceit, after the tradition of men, after the rudiments of the world, and not after Christ" (Colossians 2:8). If these "traditions" are nothing but fallen discourses, honest but erroneous attempts to express the truth as reflected in contexts that have not enjoyed the fullest light of

---

Only by comparative and promiscuous reading about individual lives embedded in other cultures can we become more aware of our embeddedness in our own.

---

revelation, perhaps culture deserves, at best, only our cautious and distant respect. But Brigham Young's audacious claim is a call for charity, to "lay hold upon every good thing" (Moroni 7:19). Charity is a Christ-centered viewpoint that requires the faith and desire to glean truths from secular sources in all cultures. In this way secular learning of culture becomes integral to the kingdom's healthy and ongoing unfolding of the restoration of all things. As the first section of the Doctrine and Covenants makes clear, God defines his commandments as divine mandates (they "are of me," he declares) even though they are also transmitted in the language of local understanding: they "were given unto my servants in their weakness, after the manner of their language" (v. 24). So while culture might be the obstacle or weakness that blinds us, it must also become the means or language by which we "might come to understanding" (v. 24). The key to this process is an uncompromised dedication to understanding God's will that links a lifelong passion for learning both from the word of God (i.e., from revelation) and from the word of men and women (i.e., from the world's cultures).

The humanities—literature, philosophy, history, and the arts—are born of a striving to bear witness to human experience in all of its varieties, often under conditions in which the particularities of experience are threatened by oblivion. Whether it is against the grain of a dictatorial political regime or of the dehumanizing forces of a consumption-obsessed economy like ours, expression in the humanities offers itself as a kind of counter-memory, one individual experience at a time, to the oblivious tendencies of power, to the passage of time, and to the persistent patterns of sin. Human expressions are rarely without sin or error, of course, but because they always demand attention to the particulars of individual lives and distinct cultures, they can provide a valuable check against our tendency to rush to quick and glib generalizations about what we deem to be the universals of human experience. If, as it has often been said, it is hard not to love someone whose story we know, it is also easy to hate or ignore someone whose story we can generalize.

The humanities also help us to see how our own particulars of cultural context have shaped our views, including our views of God. Revealed religion, of course, is by definition an expression of truth that transcends human particulars, but if we are serious in our devotion to revealed truths, it is imperative that we be mindful of how our own culture informs and shapes our understandings. Only by comparative and promiscuous reading about individual lives embedded in other cultures can we become more aware of our embeddedness in our own. Perhaps the "traditions of men" that are most dangerous are those ideologies and discourses that willfully ignore the sanctity of God's children and impetuously and impatiently bypass the responsibility of having to approach humanity one story at a time. Religious cultures are by no means inoculated from such traditions. When we speak of seeing people's true "humanity," we mean that we can see their identities as they have been shaped by time and circumstance, that we have caught a glimpse of the complexity and mystery of their inner lives, and that we feel an elemental compassion for their stories. It is equally important, of course, to see our own humanity, lest we fail to understand how we might see the world differently had we lived a different life. When the faithful disciple engages deeply with the particulars of a culture and emerges with a changed, reoriented, and enlarged vision of human experience, the humanities prove integral to the ongoing restoration of all things. Because the humanities ask us to engage in imagining the world—or in "world-making," as the word *poetics* implies—consecrated learning becomes a poetics of the Restoration.

Even if the essential ordinances and doctrines of the gospel have already been restored, the extension and application of the saving power of its doctrines depend in part on this expansion of our understanding of the broad varieties of the human condition. Because the passion, or suffering, of Christ is *compassion*— a suffering *with* all of humanity—cultivating the mind of Christ means developing an increasingly profound understanding of how the gospel relates to the diversity, range, and levels of human experience. It means learning Christ's atoning sorrow, which is an expression of understanding or feeling for the particularities of human circumstances. Thus, although the traditions of men are always a potential roadblock to understanding gospel truths, passion for the humanities founded on devotion to the Lord helps the believer to use the humanities' portrayal of those very particularities for consecrated ends. It is curious that Alma would describe a process of testing the word of God that echoes how we gain aesthetic experience. In Alma 32, especially verse 27, we find a description of the importance of a suspension of disbelief: "If ye will awake and arouse your faculties, even to an experiment upon my words, and exercise a particle of faith, yea, even if ye can no more than desire to believe, let this desire work in you." In verse 28 Alma describes a physical reaction—an enlarging of the "soul," an enlightening of "understanding," a "delicious" sensation—as long as "ye do not cast it out by your unbelief." Like art, suspension of disbelief toward the word of God yields fruit, a swelling "within your breasts; and when you feel these swelling motions, ye will begin to say within your-selves—It must needs be that this is a good seed."

Both secular and spiritual knowledge require a patient for-bearance, a willingness to allow truth to surface only after ear-nest experimentations upon the word. This kind of patient and deepened vision will not come from a superficial assessment and least of all from a cold dismissal of cultural difference. Prepara-tory for anyone to gain greater light and understanding is the cultivation of an awareness of others that keeps the soul open to mystery and wonder in the world around us and a humble accep-tance of the limits of our understanding. It is no secret to lifelong scholars that such awareness of limits only grows with time and effort. Seeking out the "best books" (Doctrine and Covenants 109:7) for anyone is a step in the direction to be able to say, like Nephi, "I know that [God] loveth his children; nevertheless, I do not know the meaning of all things" (1 Nephi 11:17). Belief in Christ, in other words, requires vigilant awareness of what we do not know and cannot be separated from a vital interest in the world, in the affairs of men and women, and in the many cultural expressions that shed light on the human experience.

Much of what I have said thus far is not exactly news in Latter-day Saint belief, even if we don't always live up to Brigham Young's challenge, but I wish to focus on why and how secu-lar learning further enables the Restoration. It is our human condition to inherit culture, so the traditions of men are going to shape and compromise the way we understand the gospel, one way or another. This is one reason why we are wise to overturn the soils of culture from time to time, lest the truths that we think we hold dear become reified, heretical, or false. Mormon explains that the intellectual purpose of charity is to "search diligently in the light of Christ that ye may know good from evil; and if ye will lay hold upon every good thing, and condemn it not, ye certainly will be a child of Christ" (Moroni 7:19). Further, Doctrine and Covenants 98:11 states, "I give unto you a commandment, that ye shall forsake all evil and cleave unto all good, that ye shall live by every word which proceedeth forth out of the mouth of God." Discipleship, in other words, is incomplete if we are merely content to forsake evil by holding on to what we already have.

The comfort and reassurance of religion sometimes appeals to the fearful, incurious, and the uncharitable mind because religion can provide an excuse to avoid the risks of learning and growing. On the other hand, discipleship is also incomplete if, in our attempt to identify and cleave unto the good in the lives of men and women, we do not maintain, as a keel and rudder on an otherwise perpetually drifting ship, an orthodox devotion to what has already been revealed. This is perhaps the fate of no small number of aspiring scholars who, willing to take notes in lecture halls and to study long hours into the night, remain unwilling to give the scriptures or the teachings of the prophets more than a cursory glance. As James reminds us, culture blinds all of us when we refuse to allow God's word to penetrate our character or when we prefer the life of ideas or convictions to a life of committed moral action (see James 1:22–23). We must resist, in other words, the temptation of assuming that it matters more to be or think right than to do good.

This is not to suggest that a disciple should be unconcerned about false ideas; this is an ongoing and real concern for any learner. But it is interesting to note what happens to ideas when they are patiently contextualized and pondered by someone living a consecrated life. Falsehood is most threatening to the mind that fears falsehood above all, especially more than it loves the good. One might think of a false idea as a common stone that some might dismiss out of hand, but others more patient might find that it retains flecks of gold. Moreover, perhaps the pursuit of ideas is less immediately about truth and error but initially an opportunity to contemplate the various forms of life and thus reflect on and even transform the nature of what we believe. Besides, there is something indecent about an uncompromis-

Learning about other cultures is vital to keeping ourselves aware of the role our own culture has played, for better or for worse, in shaping our transcendent understandings of God and ourselves.

ing pursuit of gold in a world bedecked with stones of infinite form and color! Consecration, in other words, has a tendency to unveil the world itself as the sought-after precious stone. So the effects of consecration will not be reflected so much in the content of study—which authors or artists, which period of history, culture, values, or philosophies to study—but in the amplified vision of possibility one obtains. This sacralization of knowledge means that secular knowledge gradually acquires a character that, like a window, opens the relevance of Latter-day Saint belief to wider varieties of human experience that, like a mirror, allow us to reflect on our contemporary Latter-day Saint condition.

RESTORATION AND THE TRADITIONS OF MEN

Because learning about other cultures helps us see our own culture in all its contingency and partiality, it is vital to keeping ourselves aware of the role our own culture has played, for better or for worse, in shaping our transcendent understandings of God and ourselves. Consider the ways in which their place in a particular culture and at a particular moment in history blinded Peter and his fellow disciples from understanding on the eve of Pentecost just how much more generously they needed to apply the gospel. Despite their ultimate inclusion of the Gentiles, Christ chastised the Old World disciples for their "stiffnecked-ness and unbelief" because they failed to understand how much more diverse and geographically distant the other sheep might be (3 Nephi 15:18). To have congratulated themselves merely for finally understanding that the Gentiles deserved the gospel fell short of understanding just how many "Gentiles" the world over in far away and even unknown lands qualified for the blessings of the gospel.

If it is "stiffneckedness" to have failed to imagine a people on a land mass previously unknown to the Old World, how much more unfaithful to the Lord is it for us living in this age of unprecedented access to global information to willfully ignore the particular histories, experiences, languages, and cultures of all God's children readily available to us. We rightly look forward to the prophesied day when Zion will be the envy of the world for its cultural accomplishments and secular knowledge, but we have too often imagined this would involve an immersion in our own religious uniqueness and exceptionality and our claim to have the complete treasure house of knowledge. We cannot hope to sort through the murky diversity of human experience in order to identify dangerous falsehoods if we are not equally committed to finding marvelous truths, that is, those portions of the word that the Lord has told us have been revealed across the world, to men, women, and children, according to the "heed and diligence which they give unto him" (see Alma 12:9–11; 32:23). No perpetuation of the Restoration is possible if we turn our backs on the many rich and varied traditions of men and women, the cultural achievements of the so-called heathen. Zion's greatness, I believe, will come because we will leave no stone unturned, because we have an insatiable curiosity about how others have generated ideas and lived values unique to their circumstances.

Of course, lest we lose our moorings in the process, individual devotion to the Lord's oracles is the beginning and returning point for all learning. It is also useful to remember that no one person can obtain sufficient knowledge to fully grasp the extent of the restoration of all things. In this quest, there is no room for academic, political, or cultural chauvinism, or for anti-intellectualism or fears of honest and open discussion of opinions. We don't want to be like those in Milton's day who wished to burn or ban books because they preferred an orthodoxy based on hearsay or on authority alone and not on personal witness or investigation. Milton believed that secular learning could aid in "the reforming of Reformation itself" because truth always needed further revision. "Opinion in good men," he wrote, "is but knowledge in the making."[2] For Milton the earnest Christian's

---

2. John Milton, *Areopagitica*, in *The Norton Anthology of English Literature*, ed. Stephen Greenblatt et al. (New York: W. W. Norton, 2006), 717.

duty was to hear "all manner of reason" and to commit to "books promiscuously read."[3]

In other words, Milton understood that truth had been scattered throughout the world and that its broken body must be searched for aggressively and reassembled in a gathering of insights from all books. Mormon suggests similarly that human judgment is flawed by two fundamental errors: judging that which is "evil to be of God, or that which is good and of God to be of the devil" (Moroni 7:14). Mistaking truth for error is as morally dangerous as mistaking error for truth. The countless truths that have been buried by such mistaken judgments historically have been ruinous and are arguably the very reason why art and a dispensation of restoration are necessary. As Milton notes, "Revolutions of ages do not oft recover the loss of a rejected truth, for the want of which whole nations fare the worse."[4] The only way he could imagine that we could fight against these consequences was to adopt a spirit of anticipation: "The light which we have gained was given us, not to be ever staring on, but by it to discover onward things more remote from our knowledge."[5]

Our willingness to withhold premature judgment about how ideas fit into the great expanse of God's knowledge requires charity, Christ's power to bear all things (see 1 Corinthians 13:7), which, among other benefits, strengthens us with patience to withstand the apparent contradictions of ideas, thus keeping us open to greater understanding. This openness gains direction gradually because it is framed by belief in an eventual restoration of all things, what the novelist Marilynne Robinson refers to as the "law of completion," that moment when "everything must

---

3. Milton, *Areopagitica*, 713.
4. Milton, *Areopagitica*, 712.
5. Milton, *Areopagitica*, 716.

finally be made comprehensible."[6] Without faith in this ultimate moment of circumscription of all truth to act as our compass, the partial knowledge we obtain against the great tide of chaos and forgetting that seems to be the sea we swim in would drain, instead of instill, hope. We can ill afford to be overly confident that we have arrived at a final state of understanding. Indeed, we might say that knowing an idea, feeling its truth, is a brief glimpse into a mind in which all things are known. It is as if we instinctively feel that our newfound comprehension is evidence that ideas can never be lost, even if they are often lost to our memory or changed by new information. Trust in the Restoration means that we play at secular learning, experimenting on the word long enough to harvest what fruit an idea bears.

In his monumental essay "Tradition and the Individual Talent," T. S. Eliot argues against culture's tendency to fetishize originality and uniqueness, what "least resembles anyone else," in a work of art.[7] The newness that we think we admire in a great work of art is really a function of the individual talent's ability to transmit tradition *as if* it were new. This poetics of reimagining and rearranging the past allows the individual talent to render all ages contemporaneous. Eliot notes that "not only the best, but the most individual parts of [an individual's] work may be those in which the dead poets, his ancestors, assert their immortality most vigorously."[8] These voices of the dead are displaced and reorganized by the voice of the individual talent so that new understandings emerge that simultaneously feel like things we always or once knew. It is as if to say that creating a new work of

---

6. Marilynne Robinson, *Housekeeping* (New York: Picador, 2004), 92.
7. T. S. Eliot, "Tradition and the Individual Talent," in *Selected Prose of T. S. Eliot*, ed. Frank Kermode (New York: Farrar, Straus, and Giroux, 1975), 37.
8. Eliot, "Tradition and the Individual Talent," 39.

art is really only a poetic reading, a restoration of what an earlier work of inspiration sought to express.

So one mistake we might make when we suggest that Latter-day Saints can achieve the level of accomplishment of the Bachs and Shakespeares of the world is to assume that there is a kind of radical originality in what must be accomplished. If we really believe in the Restoration, it is well to remember that as unique as we sometimes insist it is, Latter-day Saint belief is nothing new; it is the oldest understanding of the cosmos. So we could say that we already have our "Latter-day Saint" Bach: the J. S. Bach of the Brandenburg Concertos and the B-minor mass we have come to love. Not because he is or was a Latter-day Saint, of course, but because I would argue that our religion does not permit the drawing of such boundaries. There are as many Latter-day Saint writers as there are Latter-day Saint readers. That is not to say that we shouldn't aspire to Bach-like or Melville-like accomplishments, but who would want a culture without the actual Bach or Melville? Perhaps it sounds arrogant and egotistical to claim such heroes as our own, but I mean this as an expression of compassionate, not proprietary affection. If we are serious about the endeavor of gathering the house of Israel, and if all of world culture is up for grabs, Latter-day Saint culture stands to become something much more broad and inclusive, much more diverse, and much more sympathetic to the world than any of us has imagined. Indeed, it would seem that it has to if the work of restoration is to go forward.

I am persuaded that Latter-day Saint individual talent is not something that will be recognized for its uniqueness. I believe it will achieve greatness when it exhibits what Eliot calls a "continual extinction of personality" because "the poet has, not a 'personality' to express, but [becomes] a particular medium . . . in which impressions and experiences combine in peculiar and unexpected ways."[9] The goal of Latter-day Saint art or learning should not be "a turning loose," to use a phrase from Eliot, of what we have historically referred to as our Mormonism so that the whole world looks at us in envy to say that we have something special, unique, or original.[10] I suspect admiration will come when the culture of the church is truly curious about and invested in the cultures of the world, when we are seen as a people actively engaged in empathetic, disciplined conversations with other traditions, beliefs, and cultures. Eliot is suggesting a paradox that could be useful for us: the expression of religious identity could be an escape from whatever we think "Mormonism" might mean. Indeed, it might be one reason why such a word is ultimately inadequate and limiting. His idea here does not imply that greatness is achieved only when we are capable of denial or denigration of who we think we are. Not at all. As Eliot notes, "Only those who have personality and emotions know what it means to want to escape from these things."[11] In other words, the individual talent expresses itself most fully when it is adopted into the family tree of cultural achievement without compromising originality. In the terms I have been discussing, this talent is a reading of the past that is simultaneously a transmission of the old and a creation, a poetics, of something new. Unfortunately, contemporary Latter-day Saint religious culture is still very much invested in our uniqueness, still predominantly shaped by American culture and history, and still emerging from its cradle on the Wasatch Front. We are still too ambivalent about our relationship to tradition, especially the wide variety of traditions to which the restored gospel, as it spreads across the world, becomes an adopted heir.

---

9. Eliot, "Tradition and the Individual Talent," 40, 42.
10. Eliot, "Tradition and the Individual Talent," 43.
11. Eliot, "Tradition and the Individual Talent," 43.

Indeed, we seem as a culture to be at a crossroads. We are becoming increasingly international in membership, multilingual as a body and as individual members, and global in our reach. And yet we remain as closely identified as ever with a narrowly defined version of American nationalism, with a specific political party, ethnicity, and geography. This is most evident, perhaps, in the way that US Americans who descend from British Island and Scandinavian stock tend to read their own story into the Book of Mormon to the exclusion of other Americas and other Americans. Indeed, it is not yet clear that in the church's emergence out of obscurity we are doing all we can to demonstrate our commitment to listening to and gathering truth wherever it may be found. We will be like the stiffnecked disciples if we remain content with merely extending now dated and reified understandings of what we thought it meant to be "Mormon."

Our Sunday School conversations about the Book of Mormon notwithstanding, the book is *not* exclusively about Anglo-American experience within the geopolitical borders of the United States. Rather, it describes a geography in the Americas of shifting political boundaries with a plurality of cultures of various races. Surely one of its most powerful messages is its warning against geopolitical chauvinism. Nephi asks us, "Know ye not that there are more nations than one?" (2 Nephi 29:7). The Book of Mormon offers a vision of unity for that plurality, to be sure, but like the New World's greatest novels, it also issues stern warnings about the dangers of entrenched claims to identity that use force or chauvinism to achieve unity. Most significantly, it points to additional books of equal value to come forth from other lands (see 1 Nephi 13:39).

If America was the cradle of the Restoration, perhaps we would do well to consider rethinking what America means; it needn't be an ethnically narrow and geographically restricted America but rather a cross-cultural and transnational location where a dizzying variety of diasporic communities gather, commune, and influence and change each other, and thereby challenge singular ethnic or political claims on the meaning of any one nation. In other words, if it has been suggested that the Restoration took place in the United States because of its particular opportunities of religious and political freedoms, perhaps it is time to consider that American experience has also laid the groundwork for a New Jerusalem, a Zarahemla of sorts, that can become one of the great gathering places of the world's cultures: the Americas of Canada, the US, Central America, the Caribbean, and South America; the Americas of Native Americans from Tierra del Fuego to the Arctic; of Asian immigrants from Canada to Argentina; of the vast African diaspora; the Americas of Latin American, Arab, European, and other peoples of international and intranational migration. These have all yet to play their transformative role in the Restoration.

In their habits of reading and learning, some Latter-day Saints feel hesitant to embrace the educational and scholarly objectives of our politically correct and multicultural times because of today's increasing balkanization of identity and secularism. But we must be wary of the danger of a too-narrow cultural or geographical claim on eternal truth because of the ways that it isolates and excludes. Surely it is not insignificant that the Book of Mormon tells the story of immigrants, portrays the brotherhood between races, and exposes in no uncertain terms the unfinished nature of God's revelations to humankind. Indeed, the Book of Mormon implies a fundamental redefinition of the traditional Western and Hegelian conceptions of history. The book exposes the story of lost histories that are the result of sin, arrogance, and violence. It calls for greater humility and repentance in light of the ruptures and gaps in our linear understanding of the past that it portrays. Contrary to how virtually every national history has it, the structure of history, in the

Restoration at least, does not evolve by means of linear unveilings of time progressively marching from one point of origin to another point of conclusion. The linear structure that culminates in the last days is compromised by a circular returning that is implied in a Restoration, a return again to that which has been hidden since the foundation of the world in the last days.

If the Restoration is a chiasmic response to the apostasy, it would seem that the emerging knowledge of Christ throughout history spins forward but leaves behind in its wake a series of forgettings; history, in other words, results in simultaneous rupture and continuity. The Book of Mormon, for example, portrays the arrival of the Gentiles in the New World, an event that results simultaneously in the perpetuation of God's covenants *and* a loss of truth. (The Gentiles were presumably not only our British but also our Hispanic forebears. I see no reason why the Book of Mormon's account of the discovery of the Americas is not also telling the story of Hispanic Catholic colonies who, arguably more assiduously than the English Protestants, devoted extraordinary efforts to bringing the word of God to millions of the native inhabitants of the Americas.) We are told that the Gentiles receive "the power of the Lord" to defeat their mother colonies and to exercise power over the Native Americans to establish territory for themselves "out of captivity" (1 Nephi 13:16, 13). They carry with them the word of God, which contains "the covenants of the Lord" but is also missing "many parts which are plain and most precious" (1 Nephi 13:23, 26).

The results are mixed: the Gentiles are simultaneously described as "lifted up by the power of God above all other nations," and yet the fragmented truths they possess "blind the eyes and harden the hearts of the children of men" and "an exceedingly great many do stumble, yea, insomuch that Satan hath great power over them," resulting in an "awful state of blindness" (1 Nephi 13:30, 27, 29, 32). It is not always easy to see founders as both great and flawed, but that is certainly the way honest histories tell it. It is often assumed that Nephi's vision sees Columbus in a state of divine inspiration that moves him across the waters. There is little doubt from the historical record that Columbus felt so inspired, but there is also little doubt that he was blinded by a great many false traditions and ideas that caused him to fail to understand accurately where he was geographically during his voyages in the New World. This failure and his arrival had no small consequences. It is hard to see why we should celebrate Columbus's arrival unambiguously or to focus exclusively on the white immigrant story of the Americas, when in the wake of Spanish and other European arrivals, thousands of Native Americans were enslaved, only to be replaced by millions of Africans; moreover, millions of native peoples died of disease, so many that over the course of the next century and a half, the indigenous population of the Americas, estimated to be at fifty-four million before 1492, fell by almost 90 percent by the 1600s.[12]

Columbus is secondary to my main point here, which is that the Book of Mormon portrays history in the Americas as a series of events through which righteous men and women simultaneously bring the plan of God forward and (either through the failings of those same men and women or the incomplete nature of those events) leave behind pieces of the truth that need to be restored. A restoration implies a perpetual glance back, a recognition of the always-incomplete nature of human action and understanding, and a desire to find the deeper reasons for humanity's secret kinship and belonging in the covenants of Abraham. Traditional Christianity does not always fully confront these forgettings or this constant fragmentation of the gospel's truths. The restored

---

12. Shawn Miller, *An Environmental History of Latin America* (New York: Cambridge University Press, 2007), 56.

gospel posits the need for continual revolutions, that is, for continual returns to the source, to imagine again the lost connections, the repressed relations that make history less determined by evolutionary stages of the past and more determined by our imaginative acts in the present. And this poetics of restoration is the fundamental impulse of art and is reason therefore that art and culture deserve our serious attention.

Indeed, literary and historical production in the Americas, especially over the last fifty years, has shown profound interest in the early years of colonialism, the breadth and depth of more

---

> The spirit of Elijah in its broadest sense represents the search for lost knowledges in the world and the attempt to convert transgression and errantry, individuality and particularity, and bloodlines and geographies into the new substance of the story of all humankind.

---

than three centuries of African slavery throughout the Americas, and indigenous life. Moreover, the stories of immigrants and their family memories, the ethnic plurality of cities in the Americas, and the connections between the Americas and the rest of the world have figured more prominently in the literary and scholarly imagination of hundreds of writers and thinkers throughout the Americas than in any previous era of history. The stories that have emerged remind us that the great meaning of the gathering of the house of Israel is not merely blood descent but more often adoption. They suggest that the profound differences among a plurality of Americans and Americas should challenge us to imagine our kinship. This commitment to hearing scattered stories is a means of testing and potentially expanding the limits of community. It is how a poetics of restoration can avoid the pitfalls of what Edouard Glissant criticizes as an unhealthy and even violent obsession with a community's unique and sometimes hardened claims to sacred roots.[13] We see these obsessions whenever there is undue pride about the exceptional nature of a particular culture's origins or unhealthy protectionism about the purity and singularity of those origins. It is not insignificant that such negative protectionism has so often yielded to violence. Acknowledging heroism and inspired acts and words certainly enriches our understanding of the past, but acknowledging the violence, the pride, and the stumbling blocks that have also moved history forward does not diminish America. Such acknowledgement does not preclude the possibility that any nation's affairs have been providentially aided. Indeed, doing so helps us see providence in human relief. If we were to take the Book of Mormon as our inspiration, we might see a recovery of such plural and sometimes contradictory histories as our sacred duty.

Genealogy has always been effective in teaching diachronic heritage back through time but less effective in mapping the synchronic interrelatedness of communities across time. Family trees are deceptive in this regard because they stress parental links at the expense of the vast and virtually unmappable network of kinship every human being possesses across time with an innumerable family of lost cousins. The genealogical search is a discovery of kinship, but it can also be a discovery of the

---

13. Edouard Glissant, *The Poetics of Relation* (Ann Arbor, MI: University of Michigan Press, 1997).

limits of our understanding of blood, the perpetual mystery of life stories that remain beyond our grasp, and the need to supplement the inevitable lack of sufficient documentation with imagination. If there was a time when those bitten by the bug of Elijah were able to boast of their monarchic ancestors in the Old World as far back as 1066, perhaps it is time we start using genealogy to help us see our responsibilities toward our present-day kin among the far-flung races and religions of the world we inhabit.[14] To express ourselves, to know ourselves, and to be truthful to our heritage all imply that we become answerable to and interested in other peoples, other cultures, other times and places.

Who and what we imagine our community to include is often more potent than what our bloodlines indicate about our identity, and this is why culture is so important to understanding ourselves and others. If our ultimate objective is the community of the Abrahamic covenant, a binding of all the families of the earth, it is an understatement to say that there remains a lot of work to do to prepare our hearts to welcome all of God's children. Every conversion to the gospel, every consecration of one individual life, and every way of seeing the world within the framework of the great plan of happiness represents an adoption and an architectural retrofitting of the house of Israel. The spirit of Elijah in its broadest sense represents the search for lost knowledges in the world and the attempt to convert transgression and errantry, individuality and particularity, and bloodlines and geographies into the new substance of the story of all

---

14. Between 75 and 90 percent of all African Americans, for example, have white ancestry, which would suggest there are a great number of whites who either have yet to acknowledge black ancestors who may have passed as white or who have white ancestors that owned slaves and fathered children with them. See Shirlee Taylor Haizlip, *The Sweeter the Juice: A Family Memoir in Black and White* (New York: Free Press, 1995).

humankind. This spirit is operative in a disciple's secular learning because even if exposure to the particulars of another culture and identity might challenge the exceptional claims of the Latter-day Saint personality, a poetics of restoration that seeks to find the reasons for inclusion of all God's children rewards our leap of faith with a return to, not a dissipation of, the foundations of our religious identity, refreshed and restored in profoundly new ways. It is not a Tower of Babel of secular knowledge we need to build but rather the contingent scaffolding of an imagined totality that we hope the Lord will reveal beneath the stories we hear. We can never be sure we properly understand the relationships we imagine among cultures, but charity to bear all things, including for the time being what appear to be unassimilable differences, may allow us the opportunity to restore the meaning and shape of the community we hope to establish. In this sense, we are invoked as poetic creators in this ongoing restoration of all things. The aim is to remake our Latter-day Saint identity, both individually and as a culture, so as to allow more and more of the world's hidden truths to resonate in what we claim to believe, a prospect that I think bodes well for performing the great labor of the gathering of Israel and the restoration of all things.

If Truth Were a Child

This is an age of polemics. Choices are presented as mutually exclusive, and you are given little time to listen, to be reflective and careful in your judgment, or to acknowledge nuance and the validity of different points of view. You aren't even expected to present your views with any nuance, for that is considered "watering down" your message, so keep it simple, blunt, and direct, but whatever you do, don't seem to be of two minds. You are supposed to pick your enemies, not consult with or even love them. You are asked to make a choice and a quick one at that, one that binds you to one camp that is defined by its opposition to another. And it's all about identity—you are what you think, what you believe, what information you can cobble together for the sake of coherent argumentation.

For example, you either love nature or you love people, but you can't love both because to love one is to hate the other. Right now it seems that you are either sympathetic to the victims of racial profiling or sympathetic to police officers who put their lives on the line every day. Such polemics falsely pretend that to mourn the loss of life of a black man or to believe that there is such a thing as systemic racism is to hate those brave women and men who protect us, or that to understand the stress and trauma of police work is to ignore the stress and trauma of life in the streets of America for people of color. The worst offenders are the

---

Truth's value is manifest by the love we muster to build relationships in its pursuit. Its value is found in the faith it requires to hold steady in the face of uncertainty.

---

political parties, where passionate defenders have mastered the art of polemics to present us with these false choices. They seem to insist that you either believe in government or you distrust its every move. You either care about individual responsibility or you feel responsible for human society.

Such polemics have entered the logic of religious thought like an invisible toxin. You are either secular or religious. You either believe in historical change or you believe in transcendent revelation. You either believe in the infallibility of church leaders or you believe in moral relativism. You must decide to either stand up for moral truth or be compassionate toward those whose lives have taken different directions than your own, but you can't have your cake and eat it too. You either believe in the truth of your own religion or you believe that truth is everywhere or nowhere. You can't expend your energy in compassion for others while also defending God's truths. In the end, the unfortunate result of such polarized and mutually exclusive thinking is that you come to believe you are one of the good ones because now you know who the bad ones are, and good thing too you figured that out soon enough because, well, the judgment is not coming at some future point. It is already here. And of course everyone wants to be with the winners.

But the problem is that once the game is set up as a polemic, you can't win. You can't win because the rules of the game are against your becoming a whole person or seeing others as whole persons. And the rules have been in place for so long that the most vociferous among us have already made the "us versus them" mentality a lived reality. Even if you were meant to love nature *and* humanity, police officers *and* black lives, the scriptures *and* poetry, or to admire your own religion *and* the good people across this planet who will never join your faith, there is too much history suggesting that you shouldn't, that you can't. Sadly, stuck in such polemics, you won't be able to see the simultaneous reality that America has made great strides in overcoming racism or sexism and that racism and sexism are still alive and well. You won't be able to admit the blessings of secularism while also claiming to be religious. All you can do is hold up your corner of truth.

But that's just it. All we possess is a corner, a piece, not the whole of it. Truth is no trophy in our glass case or award framed on our wall. Its value isn't in possessing it. Reality certainly doesn't have only two sides, one true and one false. As I have insisted earlier, truth's value is manifest by the love we muster to build relationships in its pursuit. Its value is found in the faith it requires to hold steady in the face of uncertainty and questions that inevitably arise when we finally have the humility to understand how much of it eludes us. This is why we need God and each other—even our enemies—to teach us truth. And what we gain isn't some fact or thing. We gain experiences and relationships that teach us love. The pursuit of truth tethers us to each other and to God, and when we hold up our corner in our zealous impatience to possess the whole of it, we not only risk ignoring the entire fabric as a result but we imperil our relationships. This is why we have "patriots" who wish to shoot federal officers, fathers and mothers who will shun family members to protect their idea of family, champions of political or religious truth who will trample their own values—and the most vulnerable among us along the way—just for the sake of being right, thus becoming self-proclaimed stewards of the earth who nevertheless deem it their duty to lay waste to the land. The apostle Paul made it clear: we can have the truth, but if we don't have charity we have nothing (1 Corinthians 13:1–3). And we don't have charity, said Jesus, until we love our enemies (Matthew 5:44). There is no point in wondering if we are in error, because we are.

Now wait a minute, you insist. That all sounds too wishy-washy. What about that scriptural metaphor we find so often that describes the word of God as a sword that cuts deep to the bone? After all, the Lord told Joseph Smith, "Behold, I am God; give heed unto my word, which is quick and powerful, sharper than a two-edged sword, to the dividing asunder of both joints and marrow; therefore give heed unto my words" (Doctrine and Covenants 6:2). Here the word of God separates. It does the work of cleaning the animal, of separating the viscera from the muscle, the muscle from the bone, the skin from the fat. It is violent. It demands a decision. "Choose you this day," right? (Joshua 24:15). We can't afford to sit on fences. Jesus himself prophesied that he would bring division and that he who was unwilling to leave family was unworthy of him (Luke 14:26). If Jesus is the word that heals, that feeds the hungry soul, that slakes our thirst, isn't he also the sword that cuts to the quick?

POLEMICS OF THE SELF

Good questions, all. When I have wrestled with my own sins and find myself in a prolonged delay of my repentance, it is usually because I have imagined the sword of justice in abeyance. I can tell myself: I can choose tomorrow, but no need to do so today. I figure that my heart and circumstances are far more complex for proper reckoning, that there is no reason to act with undue urgency, and that ambiguity is all. But then it hits. Something triggers the feeling that I should take the Lord at his word. I might try to protest. I wasn't intent on rebellion, I say. I was just exploring or being lazy or just not deciding yet because, you know, there's lots of truth out there. Give me time, Lord! What's the hurry? Why so much threatening language? But when I take him at his word and allow right and wrong to become more clearly distinct in my mind, I feel the full weight of the word's urgency. I allow it to do its work. Over and over it says, "Repent. Don't delay."

For me this moment of mini-judgment is what the scriptures describe as the "fear of the Lord." We are squeamish about this idea, maybe because it seems so judgmental, so harsh. It might trigger something like shame or self-hatred, especially when we realize our sins have accumulated and made us repeat offenders. We may be tempted to wonder if we simply aren't cut out for this gospel living. From my experience, that's when it feels like the finger of the Lord is just pointing or shaking at me in disgust and delayed repentance seems like the only option. But such anxiety and shameful fear should tell me something about where such feelings are coming from—they signal my failure to comprehend the truth of God's mercy. I might try to convince myself that the mistake is to believe in right and wrong in the first place, but the real mistake is in believing that *I* am only either right or wrong and that there is something preordained or prescribed in this whole game of trying to figure out who I am in my essence, as if my identity is a fate to be discovered. I am truly trapped in sin when I think of my actions or my thoughts as evidence I have been discovered for the failure or success that I am, that I lose or win, and that I will do one or the other.

But who we are is neither inherently good or bad but loved and inherently free, capable of becoming perfected and whole like God, with God. All of us.

As I have aged and become more familiar with the experience of confronting my failings, I now understand the urgency of God's word differently. Mini-judgment days must arrive and I must respond, but not because God is angry and has had enough but because allowing myself to feel urgency is the only way I can access God's power to help me change. I simply have to decide if I am with him or against him, if I am primarily interested in obedience or in rebellion. In such moments of accountability, I can see the risks I have taken in delaying my decision to really love the Lord with all my heart. When I truly believe, I give heed and the word divides me, or better said, it shows me that I am divided. And at that point I am willing to place my sins on the altar. Perhaps, then, this desire is a result of the carving work performed all along by the word-as-sword, helping me to see myself more accurately.

Okay, you say, now you are getting morbid! The Lord wants to cut me up and place me on an altar? Well, perhaps think of it this way: you and I need clarity. We need to see ourselves in proper perspective so we can properly assess where we are and where we have been. Then God wants us to see ourselves as we can become, to be sanctified, made holy, which is the same meaning of the word *sacrifice*.

So the metaphor is reworked: instead of cutting you up and apart, he is preparing you for a refashioning. He doesn't want to throw you out or even parts of you. He wants all of you—your desires for God, your talents and gifts, as well as your senseless lusts and vanities, your petty feelings of jealousy and hurt. But in order to have all of you, he needs you to accept responsibility for your whole story and how divided you are, based on when you betray or contradict yourself. He wants you to find a way to become united, to bring your past, all your mistakes, your entire life story into some beautiful remade vision of eternal possibility and goodness. Like every great artist who has looked into the abysses of human history in order to create meaning, Christ takes the nightmare of your darkest hours and transforms them into a vision of possibility. There is no way you are doing that on your own. You know this already. That's why you hate parts of yourself, why you fear being seen in your nakedness, why the

Christ's word asks you to see yourself with pity and with compassion as you might look upon a beautiful newborn. This means that you must learn how to be reborn in Christ, to become *his* child, allowing him to help you see yourself as he sees you.

thought causes so much shame. But what if, instead of imagining these as the undesirable parts of yourself, you understood that you need to own these parts of yourself in order for you to become a whole person, fully consecrated to the Lord? Is that why the Lord goes searching for those parts?

Wouldn't you prefer this? This isn't merely a matter of preferring the good aspects over the bad aspects of yourself. It requires something far deeper. It requires charity, Christ's pure love, for yourself because of its power to bear all things that you have experienced, all the things you have ever said or done, so as to enable you to decide that you can accept the whole of it and present it as your offering to the Lord. Christ's word is quick, which means it is alive, and it sees you not as component parts but as a living whole. His word asks you to see yourself with pity and with compassion as you might look upon a beautiful newborn. This means that you must learn how to be reborn in Christ, to become *his* child, allowing him to help you see yourself as he sees you. With the alchemical power of his atonement and its potent combination of justice and mercy, Christ takes you—all of you—and transforms you.

So when factions today compete for your attention and loyalty and claim to possess the truths to help you discover your identity, remember that your potential—sustained by God's love—is the truth you are trying to discern, and God's word is the power to provide this revelation. When he reveals things to you, when he answers your prayers, he gives you far more than a nugget of truth. He gives a relationship that isn't merely a reward for being who you are but the power to change and become like him. He himself is first and foremost what he always reveals— his love and his knowledge of your life. If you are burdened by questions or consumed by criticism of others, his loving presence may answer some of those questions, and if not, it will provide the sustaining hope you need to live with those burdens.

If you listen to the book of Hebrews where this language about the sharp edges of God's word first appears, you learn that the author is suggesting that the only way you are going to throw yourselves into the arms of the living God is if you have faith that you will not, in fact, be chopped up, spit out, or otherwise cast away, but instead healed. Hebrews follows this description of the word's sharp edges by explaining that the word is also "a discerner of the thoughts and intents of the heart" (Hebrews 4:12). More like a scope than a weapon, the word is doing the work of discernment, of diagnosis. God wants to help you figure out what you really want so that once confronted with the evidence of where your heart currently is, you might understand why you might want to choose a higher way. Christ doesn't *discover* your intentions. He knew them all along; *he is trying to help you see them*: "Neither is there any creature that is not manifest in his sight: but all things are naked and opened unto the eyes of him with whom we have to do." And there is more: "For we have not an high priest which cannot be touched with the feeling of our infirmities; but was in all points tempted like as we are, yet without sin. Let us therefore come boldly unto the throne of grace, that we may obtain mercy . . . to help in time of need" (Hebrews 4:13, 15–16). God understands how hard it can sometimes be to sort out motivations, to understand why you persist in sin even when you know better, why you can never quite seem to become the person you most want to become.

So all of this division is the result not of being carved up, but of finally being able to discern yourself and your contradictions, and this vision prepares your flesh to be placed on the sacrificial altar whereby your sins are, by the refiner's fire, annealed and converted into whole strengths. Alma similarly urges, "Do not endeavor to excuse yourself in the least point because of your sins, by denying the justice of God; but do you let the justice of God, and his mercy, and his long-suffering have full sway in your heart; and let it bring you down to the dust in humility" (Alma 42:30). Notice he wants not just God's justice but his mercy and long-suffering as well to have "full sway." If his justice helps you see the truth of what you have done, his mercy reassures you that that truth does not define or limit what you can become. And the truth is that—unlike the polemical division of everything and everyone into clear categories of right and wrong, good and bad—we are, all of us, a mix of both. For this reason we cannot see ourselves properly or make proper judgments of reality without believing in both his justice—his reasons for condemning us—and his mercy—his reasons for forgiving and healing us. Such faith allows God to do his alchemy of making our weaknesses strong, making our complexity whole, coherent, directed, and aided in a process of sanctification. As the world clamors for our attention, we do well to remember that we don't need coherent arguments so much as self-coherence, and until and unless we give our attention to this essential work of knowing and healing ourselves, our arguments about the world and all of its problems are likely to be based on faulty perception. In other words, our tendency to see the world polemically is a symptom of our failure to see ourselves and others wholly. Getting this right is lifelong labor. There is both comfort and urgency in the thought that the jury is always out on us. In the meantime, we can think of judgment as a hot coal. Christ has warned to keep ourselves at a distance.

And for good reason. The mind is a changeable thing and not always the most reliable filter by which to perceive reality. I recognize, of course, that this is somewhat of an odd statement, since it is hard to imagine how else we might be able to perceive reality except through our own minds. One of my favorite paintings is by René Magritte, called *The Human Condition*. In it he thematizes the paradox of trying to see the world beyond the constraints of how our eye and imagination already see it. If we were able to see beyond the frame through which our unique capacities for perception are able to see, he seems to say, we would still see the world in the same way. We can't imagine what we can't imagine. We cannot, in other words, fully escape or transcend ourselves. It might seem at first counterintuitive, but I believe this is precisely why I need to rely on God. I rely on God because I can't fully trust myself. I can't even fully trust my capacity to understand or perceive who he is or what he wants. So faith is both a trust in God's light to assist me and a distrust in my own capacity to make sense of things. To be religious means I must be willing continually to self-examine and self-question.

And upon self-examination, I have to admit that my world-views and attitudes seem to change according to my mood, and my mood, although a fickle thing, is generally shaped by how I am living. Doubts are not necessarily the fruit of sin. One can be good and obedient and still struggle with belief. And one can believe and still sin. In fact, we all sin, but precisely for that reason we must adopt a lifestyle of repentance if we are to avoid constructing too much of a world, a god, and a self-image that conform to our most base desires. My experience tells me that improved perception—seeing more truly and more clearly—comes with improved and more disciplined commitment to the commandments of God. To be obedient to God's word will not free us from the responsibility to wager our best judgments amid uncertainty or from questions, but as I have suggested, it will at least aid us in gaining clarity about and power over ourselves.

Seeing that I always seem to live in a state of imperfect devotion to God's will, I find it easy to become swayed either by utter and total self-rejection or, on the contrary, by values and beliefs that would justify me in my sinfulness. What am I going to do to get rid of the irritation that is always coming from my conscience? Will I finally have enough discipline to conquer myself and all bad habits, or will I feel forced to generate new beliefs that justify my current choices? How long can I persist in striving to overcome a bad habit that doesn't want to go away? On what basis can I continue to feel good about myself if I can't ever quite conquer all of my weaknesses? Without Christ's charity for ourselves, without feeling his abiding love for my inherent worth and his perfect willingness to forgive even in the midst of our hypocrisies, small or large, it is difficult to continue to believe in gospel standards and live in a state of friction with myself for very long. But consider how many worldviews are designed to justify a selfish will. What a tragedy it would be to have spent a life and held to a philosophy that were both bent by appetite.

What amazes me is how often simple questions about how and what I eat, what self-image I have, how often I judge others by their physical appearance, how I think about sexuality and act on my sexual appetites, and what I think about material possessions can all directly influence my ability to have faith in God, to feel charity for others, and to be at my best intellectually. These questions of my own carnality seem to be foundational to how my mind works, what it chooses to perceive, what it wants to ignore, and how much hope I feel about my life in particular and life in general. Consistently and perhaps not surprisingly, I find that the greater self-control I can muster and the more respect and reverence I can feel for my own body and the bodies of others, truth appears more rich, complex, and ubiquitous and the world is more interesting, beautiful, and meaningful.

In Christianity we call these feelings the fruits of the Holy Spirit. They are God's way of teaching us how to live and assisting us in the quest for deep and lasting happiness despite our weaknesses. There are two facts about me that are perpetually true: I am never living exactly as I ought, and God's love and my inherent worth never change. I believe that the fellowship of my church is designed to help broken people and that I need the encouragement of church life to engage in good living to be happy, so I am grateful for a community that assists me, motivates me, and reinforces the good choices I need to be making every single day about my body and the bodies of others. I understand it doesn't always work that way for others. I would only suggest that a vague and general distrust of the body of The Church of Jesus Christ of Latter-day Saints and of other institutions and people might simplify life, but it will do little to help us more truly see ourselves. Withdrawal and separation are sometimes necessary to avoid an abusive and toxic situation, but a philosophy that is grounded in radical, individual autonomy and profound distrust of institutions does not strengthen an ability to live in community. We are beholden to and responsible for not only our own body but the bodies of family and friends and those of my enemies, my community, my nation, and the populations of the world. They are also the bodies of plants and animals, the very body of the earth. We are in a moral economy, and each and every day I make decisions as a consumer and as a citizen in a plural society about how I will use my body and interact with the bodies of others, and these choices add up to who I am morally and spiritually. If I can see only my own body, even if I am good at respecting it, I am failing to understand myself and the full extent of my stewardship. As the Lord revealed to Joseph Smith in section 49 of the Doctrine and Covenants:

> For, behold, the beasts of the field and the fowls of the air, and that which cometh of the earth, is ordained for the use of man for food and for raiment, and that he might have in abundance. But it is not given that one man should possess that which is above another, wherefore the world lieth in sin. And wo be unto man that sheddeth blood or that wasteth flesh and hath no need.

The Lord seems to be calling for an equitable and modest treatment of all flesh, both human and more-than-human, and as is evident in other scriptures, this pertains to our capacity to take life in order to sustain ourselves, to generate life through sexual union, and to either nurture or harm the lives that come into our care. There is no room here for seeing ourselves above others or for seeing other people or even material possessions as objects, things to be possessed or used for merely selfish gain or things to be ignored. We should see them instead as "living souls" with whom we might commune and collaborate in the interest of the health of the entire community of life. It is little wonder that what awakes me from spiritual stupor is invariably a sudden reminder of the soulful presence of another, whether it be the glance I steal at my wife while she sleeps next to me and I suddenly feel flooded with love or those moments of discovery that my children are far more complex and beautiful and individual than I had realized. It might be an experience with music or literature where I am lifted up high enough to see a broader landscape of humanity around me or when I have lifted myself up onto a mountain and can catch a better glimpse of the immensity and diversity of this planet. These are all moments in which I discover that I am one living soul among many. Rather than making me feel crowded or burdened in the midst of such presences, the wound of my own solitude is healed and I feel something of what the Creator feels for all life. Even if I still "see through a glass, darkly" (1 Corinthians 13:12), I know in those moments that I see more clearly and more rightly. I will never overcome all my weaknesses, and I will never see perfectly, at least not in this life. It took me years to understand that this shouldn't bother or deter me in my pursuit of proper insight, and knowing I won't quit trying and that the Lord won't stop loving me has given me great confidence and peace.

POLEMICS IN THE CHURCH

Although the Christian religion expects repentance and upholds standards of right and wrong, it isn't true Christian religion but the partisan pressures of today—on the left as much as on the right—that distort Christian values as if in a funny mirror and demand judgment precisely in moments and circumstances where Christian forbearance is needed. I suppose this is why many in society today want a moratorium on the harsh and judgmental tones of many prominent Christian voices and why many members of The Church of Jesus Christ of Latter-day Saints feel pressure from friends and family who are not religiously inclined to have an answer for every social issue. Christians are prone to overstate their own injustices, I have observed, but that does not preclude the phenomenon of religious zeal among those disenchanted with religion. I wonder why anyone should believe they need to have answers for everything. I don't much respect faith when it crowds out reflective

> ## Because I am an agent striving to become a more fully realized version of myself, belief in a God made manifest through revelations requires me not only to cling to what I know but to live with questions.

thought and use of reason, but I also find myself suspicious of demands to have all the answers or of claims to have them, especially in cases where a simple "I don't know" would suffice. Knowing when to say "I don't know" is as virtuous as knowing when to say "I love you." We ought not to be uncomfortable or unfamiliar with either sentence.

It is understandable to expect a revealed religion to conform to reason, and even setting aside for a moment the unusual claims of the church regarding golden plates and angelic visitations, Latter-day Saints often act and speak as if living the gospel were an entirely rational proposition. But I want to ask why we have elevated the individual powers of reason and individual conscience above all other considerations. I don't mean to sound anti-intellectual or dismissive of the sacred nature of individual conscience. Rationality and individual integrity have become highly valued virtues for good reason. But it seems the fundamental ideal of revealed religion isn't merely to be true to myself but to seek the marriage of individual will with the will of God. Besides, to which "self" or part of one's self would one choose to be loyal? How would I know that it is my best self? How could I be sure that I'm not making an idol out of some idea of myself or of the cosmos that justifies rather than seeks to correct and improve how I behave? The objective of revealed religion, it seems to me, is an integrity that binds believers to God—and not just an internal integrity claimed on the basis of loyalty to an idea. Even the great ally of reason can be compromised by motives and vanities I may not yet discern. So as rational as I like to think my faith is, it isn't always rational, nor do I suspect I should demand it to be.

Because I am an agent striving to become a more fully realized version of myself, belief in a God made manifest through revelations requires me not only to cling to what I know but to live with questions. My relationship to what I know is never static. It requires vigilance and patience, love and fidelity, and it requires me to be open to but not to lose undue sleep over questions. To paraphrase Emily Dickinson, questions can keep my faith nimble and alive, but only if I am motivated more by trust than by fear.[1] For this reason, it seems paramount that we create in our homes and in our wards a trusting environment that is conducive to asking and exploring questions as we assist one another to become grounded in the fundamentals of a testimony. Speaking to Latter-day Saint youth leaders in 1934, Elsie Talmage Brandley suggested that if we focus on teaching and

---

1. Dickinson wrote, "We both believe, and disbelieve a hundred times an Hour, which keeps Believing nimble." Letter 750, 30 April 1882, http://archive.emilydickinson.org/correspondence/lord/l750.html.

nurturing the basics, we can avoid making "the word of God grounds for unnecessary misunderstanding."[2] Those basics consist of the divinity of Christ, the divinely instigated restoration of the gospel and its scriptures, and the divine right of General Authorities to speak in the name of God and be special witnesses of Christ. Pleading with leaders to listen to the questions posed by youth, she added: "To the fundamental roots of church belief we cling; to them we anchor our faith; in them we believe. Differences which may arise between groups and individuals are not based upon these roots. Outside of this, which is basic, opinions may diverge. As leaders, let us examine possible evidences of differences and reasons for them, if they exist, and try to glimpse a possible solution."[3]

It is a risk and perhaps a danger to attach ideological baggage to the core teachings of the gospel, whether it comes from secular humanism or free market economics. I suppose too that, given our tendency to see askew, it is inevitable that we will never perfectly and clearly perceive the fundamental purity of the gospel. But our weakness as culturally mediated beings can become our strength if we allow the free play of questions and exploration in and around the core principles of the gospel and we do so in faith that the revelations will yet reveal more to our understanding with more and better questions. Consider the status of Isaiah's revelations and how it took generations to understand how they pertained to his time, to the time of Nephi, and to ours, simultaneously. If Latter-day Saints believe all that the Lord has revealed and all that he has yet to reveal (Articles of Faith 1:9), perhaps some future revelations will come just from rereading what we already have for its deeper import. Consider too Joseph F. Smith's experience of rereading 1 Peter 3:19 in light

---

2. Elsie Talmage Brandley, "The Religious Crisis of Today," *At the Pulpit* (Salt Lake City: Church Historian's Press, 2017), 139.
3. Brandley, "Religious Crisis of Today," 138.

of the deaths of World War I and the influenza outbreak and coming to understand the great work for the dead (Doctrine and Covenants 138). This is why I believe that it is valuable to treat the questions that emerge in contemporary society with respect and seriousness and not dismissively or derisively, but also why it is important to learn some patience and not demand or expect things inside the church to always conform to the way things are done elsewhere.

There are inevitable tensions between the status of God's revelations and contemporary culture, and those tensions don't always resolve or resolve in the way our political leanings might prefer. This isn't always fun or easy to explain to others. It doesn't satisfy a lot of people. But I have learned through sad experience that I have wasted vital spiritual energy needed for my own self-reformation by worrying myself too much about the gap between the way the church does things and the way the world seems to expect it to. If it is indeed a revealed religion, things will happen on the Lord's time and according to his will, which is another way of saying that we all run the risk of misinterpreting God's purposes. This might mean for believing critics that more patience and forbearance are required, just as it might imply for believing defenders the need to create safe places for earnest and honest questions. Such spaces have been vital to the growth and development of the church. Again, as Elsie Talmage Brandley so presciently and wisely stated, "Is there a place—a legitimate and reverent place—for inquiry in the building of a testimony? We answer—we *must* answer—yes, and say that the basis of doubt and inquiry has been the genius of the church, the power through which members have fought their way into it."[4]

We cannot afford to shame people for having doubts or for offering fair and needed criticisms. The last thing the church

---

4. Brandley, "Religious Crisis of Today," 141–42.

needs is passivity from its members, but the health and vitality of the living church does need sufficient faith and respect for what we do know the Lord has revealed. It certainly means forbearance when confronted with a fellow faithful church member who sees things differently. Sometimes revelations take time, multiple witnesses, and further light before they become more clear in our minds. In the meantime, it pays not to get overworked when one can't make sense of things. This patience means being willing to live with and suffer through contradictions in the short term. In the long term, patience helps to make more sense of revelation, but it also most importantly brings more peace.

In our relationship in and with institutions, it is hard to argue that patience is always a virtue. I certainly don't believe it is a categorical one. One has to weigh these considerations carefully and individually, but it only seems fair to offer the same patience to others that we would hope for ourselves. Let me speak personally for a moment. Because I have seen how profoundly my judgment can be skewed by my own sins, for me it became imperative to remain faithful to my covenants. Without them, I am vulnerable to my weaknesses. With them, I have the security to explore ideas with greater trust as well as the sacred obligation to listen to and serve others. I used to feel ashamed at my need for continual repentance and searching and reaching for Christ's power to lift me up to meet the demands his truths want to make of me, but now I see that this struggle keeps me focused on being as true to truth as I am on knowing it. In that way I have found I am less likely to allow a problem with the institutional church or with my local ward to infect my access to the peace that surpasses understanding (see Philippians 4:7). Working to unite my will to the Lord's is work enough for a lifetime, in any case, and at least one way to avoid letting institutional and cultural baggage get in the way of my goal of remaining humble and teachable. So what I want to suggest simply is the value of keeping our fundamental tasks front and center—that of reconciling our will to God's, of bringing souls to Christ, bringing healing to others, building up their faith, loving them, seeing the best in them, and loving and serving God with joy. In this way we may not have any more answers than we would otherwise, but we will have a much happier life and a deeper kind of integrity.

POLEMICS OF THE CHURCH IN THE WORLD

Others who believe differently than we do will have answers, and some of them might be worth embracing. As described earlier, it is essential to remain faithful to the fundamentals, but the totality of God's revelations is not like a science textbook, so I see no reason why we can't be open to science's findings and insights. I know of no official Latter-day Saint interpretation of, say, the significance of abolition or of contemporary civil rights. I have principles and values to guide me, but I am also encouraged to learn from history, literature, political philosophy, and science. I know of no doctrinal basis for concluding that we have all truth already in our possession and that we can therefore forsake the responsibility to educate ourselves continually and carefully about all matters pertaining to God's kingdom. And no reason to believe, for that matter, that there are limits to what kind of knowledge is relevant and what is not.

So enormous is this task of learning that it raises questions about the viability and need for apologetics, at least of the sort that sees itself limited to entrenched warfare. The truths of the restored gospel are indeed often misunderstood, under attack, or simply ignored, but it is as important to avoid understating what we know as it is to avoid overstating it. It seems that I say as much about my faith in Christ and in the restored gospel by my generosity of thought, my curiosity, and my openness to correction as I do by my willingness to stand up for what I believe in and far more, certainly, than any defensiveness or aggressive intellectual takedowns of others. If the church or its doctrines need defense, it may be because of a shortage of solid reasoning and public articulation of such reasoning. But reasoning alone will not persuade more people. When a defender appears to care more about protecting the right view of a matter than about living up to the high demands of her own beliefs, then she is less likely to be persuasive. Moreover, if the doctrines are indeed true, the risk isn't that they won't have power in the world but that you and I will fail to understand them or defend them properly. Even when defensiveness is intended to be an act of love, if it is seen otherwise, another strategy would help. A posture that is only defensive and cannot admit the value of listening to criticism is only interested in self-justification. The gospel's restored doctrines have wide-ranging implications, and for that reason they require proper humility, self-questioning, and generosity. These qualities will do as much or more to help the doctrines realize their fullest implications in society than any amount of argumentation. I would welcome a moratorium on sectarian defensiveness.

I suppose my attitude is informed by my sense as an educator that we are still not done with the great restoration of all truth. Nothing has caught my imagination quite like those grandiose statements of Brigham Young such as this one: "'Mormonism,' so-called, embraces every principle pertaining to life and salvation, for time and eternity. No matter who has it. If the infidel has truth it belongs to 'Mormonism.' The truth and sound doctrine possessed by the sectarian world, and they have a great deal, all belong to this church. As for their morality many of them are morally just as good as we are."[5] This isn't an arrogant assumption that we own all truth already. On the contrary, it is

---

5.   Brigham Young, in *Journal of Discourses* (London: Latter-day Saints' Book Depot, 1867), 11:375 (April 8, 1867).

a call of great humility and dedication to learning of all kinds done in the spirit of faith in Christ and charity toward all. The restoration of the church through Joseph Smith brought us fundamentally important knowledge; however, it didn't finish but rather began the restoration of all things. It gave us the tools, the essential covenants, by which we might continue the ongoing labor of restoration. If our truths need defense, I have to believe that all forms of learning will only benefit our capacity to live and articulate the truths of the gospel and allow them to flourish in society much more effectively than mere defensiveness and negative protectionism. The gospel is the good news of God's love for the world, and that love is manifest in us by our willingness to seek and embrace truth wherever it may be found. Such a spirit of learning seems as essential a defense of our faith as anything else. If there is a need for apologists, I suppose they would be most effective by being aggressive and proactive in gathering truth, rather than in merely protecting truth from distortion. Such protectionism seems counter to what I understand faith in the truth to be because it seems to insist, *contra* faith, that how we currently understand things is sufficient and adequate to the truths we uphold.

The fact that the body of truth seems to have been scattered throughout the world, on one hand, might make it seem foolish to believe in and be loyal to the exclusive claims of any one religion, least of all one that claims to be the "only true and living church" (Doctrine and Covenants 1:30). But if I am serious about being loyal to truth, I see no reason to believe that I will succeed in gathering the body of truth if I think I'm required to drop one truth in order to grasp another, as if there is only so much room for truth. The fact of scattered truths, on the other hand, might threaten believers if they think of truth as a zero-sum game—that is, if they think that any claim of a new truth somehow waters down or diminishes instead of ennobles and brightens what has already been revealed. It isn't my church that has been the chief source of understanding about, say, the mechanisms by which life emerged on this planet, for example, or about the realities of human trafficking and genocide today. That isn't to say that these issues matter more than the atonement of Christ or his covenants, but it is to say I need not fear or devalue ideas and concerns that emerge elsewhere, on one hand, or imagine that their importance disqualifies the claims of the restored gospel, on the other. What we read in the papers and

Being right is not as important, nor as satisfying, as being good. Our work is to re-member, to build community and provide belonging in God for all of God's children.

what we study in the cultures of the world only provide new contexts in which we can discover perhaps stronger understandings of divine revelation and the broad reach of divine love, but only if we are willing to let new information help us formulate new questions. This is exciting work and far more rewarding than if we spent the better part of our Christian energy identifying and denouncing the falsehoods of another religion or other worldviews. Besides, in such cases history shows that it can take generations to recover from our mistaken judgments, not to mention the bad precedent we might set by rushing to judgment before we have done the work of identifying and embracing the common ground we share with others. To put Paul's admonition in the simplest of terms, unless I am primarily motivated by charity, my judgment is likely to make a mess of things (see 1 Corinthians 13:1–2). Being right is not as important, nor as satisfying, as being good. Our work is to re-member, to build community and provide belonging in God for all of God's children. We cannot afford to let wrangling over concepts become more important than our relationships with others or with God.

The famous story of King Solomon's wisdom embodies what I have wanted to say here. The first test of the king's wisdom was a polemic. A child dies. The mother, in her grief, believes she can find a substitute for her living child by stealing another. She and the mother of the stolen child, each adamant that the child is hers, appeal to the king to resolve their differences. Solomon's words are chilling: "Divide the living child in two, and give half to the one, and half to the other" (1 Kings 3:25). Didn't Jesus say something similar? Didn't he say we had to choose the truth and forsake error? That we had to find a way to either be with him or against him? How can this be? Sometimes I am, sometimes I am not. Although I am commanded to remember him always, I *never* remember him always. I am never on his side *at all times.* Sometimes I find myself wanting what is wrong, or judging the poor, hating my enemy, lusting after things or people to possess, failing time and time again to see and love others as complex flesh-and-bone human beings in all their mystery and wonder. Am I doomed? Is everyone else? If I must choose, as the gospel demands, but I can't stick with my choice perfectly, am I a hypocrite?

Maybe, but perhaps if I accept my foolishness and learn trust and love and humility, maybe this is a truer choice than expending all of my energy just so I can assert that I am one of the good guys, that I have already and always made the right choices.

The two women face the impossibility of dividing the truth in two. The woman who is blinded by her pain is willing to divide the child in order to persist in her lie. She thus becomes a living contradiction—she is willing to lose the very thing she desires just so that she can have it dead. But that is what she wanted all along: a divided child instead of a living child, a living soul, a body to which she is answerable. A living child cannot be owned, bounded, or kept from others. She was wrong to believe that there could be an adequate substitute for a living body. The woman who knows and loves her child can see only one choice. She must give up the child to the other woman so that it can remain whole and alive. She has this courage because all along a living being is what she loved and understood could not be replaced. Her love of the child means she must let go of the need to be right so that she can do what is good. Only in this way can the fleshy, indivisible truth in the form of the child's body be preserved. The cost, of course, is giving the child up altogether. Solomon's attempt to divide the truth tests her mettle and reveals the truth of her love. She is revealed as the true mother because hers is the true love, and so the child is returned (1 Kings 3:26–27). The Christian message of the story is the promise of restoration. Solomon's wisdom is God's mercy, a recompense for sacrificing the pride of being right in order to be good.

So it raises the question, with how much more care and humility would we speak and act if the truth were not the result of some game of words or a battle of wills, but a flesh-and-bone living child, a living soul? What if we thought of the truth as something that couldn't be owned or divided up into broken pieces but was instead something we had to learn to gather and keep together with love? Maybe all truth in the end is measured against the lives of children. It is worth remembering that a living child is, in fact, the form in which the Truth came to us.

Letter to
a Remarkable Student

I don't know about you, but I move back and forth, almost like a perpetual tide, between a desire to see the world as standing in need of radical change and a desire to caution myself against believing in the correctness of my own judgment and to instead learn to look more carefully and patiently at what life presents to me and to learn from it. As the author E. B. White once humorously said, "I arise in the morning torn between a desire to improve (or save) the world and a desire to enjoy (or savor) the world. This makes it hard to plan the day."[1] Given our tendency to accept and even justify a status quo that is harmful and insufficient, I am convinced that we all must change, and yet I also feel a nagging and honest feeling that deep self-scrutiny is always necessary. Sometimes this pendulum swing feels like cowardice and sometimes like a virtue—which is to say, like everyone else I suppose, my disposition is both a weakness and a strength.

---

1. Quoted in a profile by Israel Shenker, "E. B. White: Notes and Comment by Author," *New York Times*, July 11, 1969.

You may have noticed that we all have tendencies to imagine the world in a certain way and then we spend a great deal of our time bumping up against the worlds others have imagined differently. This can be a source of great strife in our lives and even loneliness. Sometimes we have that magical experience of finding like-minded people who seem to occupy the same planet we do. We become fast friends, and this is a great source of joy.

> Repentance and education are ways of life, not one-time affairs. We are never done repenting and never done educating ourselves.

But, of course, sometimes people surprise us. The most unlikely of people can become sources of great inspiration or solace. And the world surprises as well. Although it can be a source of great sorrow to discover we were wrong about the world, it is exciting to learn and grow into a world that is more complex and diverse than we had thought. This provides a much-needed source of wisdom.

What I want to say is that we are all poetic by nature. We are world-makers. We receive information from the world that makes claims on us about what is real and true and what is fake and false, and with varying degrees of self-conscious awareness, we repurpose that information and project a worldview of our own making that gives meaning to our lives. Some of us, of course, are very bad poets, as it were, because we have not learned the self-awareness that constitutes all great art. We do

not develop enough awareness of the limits of what we understand, we do not listen to others, and we never grow. We retreat
from the challenge of moving and changing maps by recourse
to dogmatic denial, fear, and stubbornness. Actually, it might
be more accurate to say that on some level all of us are at least
not yet great poets and that we all make these mistakes to some
degree or another.

Indeed, the real danger, I suppose, is that at some point as
we gain more enlightenment about the world we stop question-
ing ourselves and imagine that we are not as determined by our
circumstances as others, that the worldview we hold is genuine,
well-informed, authentically made. Of course, as a religious person and as an educator in the humanities, I place a lot of hope
in the idea of change and in the possibility of enlightenment.
Repentance and education are both essential requirements, but
repentance and education are ways of life, not one-time affairs.
We are never done repenting and never done educating ourselves. It always seems to me to be the case, as literary history
has proved, that no great poet, no matter how accomplished, is
very far from writing a really bad poem. For that matter, no great
theologian is incapable of being deeply mistaken about matters,
no scientist incapable of making the most disastrous judgments,
and no man or woman, no matter how righteous or smart or
profoundly good, is without blind spots, weaknesses, and error.

There is a great scramble in our society today to avoid ever
being deceived, to avoid the embarrassment of ever being wrong.
Beware of this. You will be wrong. You and I are wrong about
many things right now. We should want to embrace the truth,
of course, but precisely for this reason we should be dedicated to
a lifelong process of change. Otherwise we mistakenly assume
we already have all we need. And it seems that if the Book of
Mormon makes one point emphatically clear it is that self-
confidence in having enough truth is a great sin. But this great

scramble for confidence has polarized us into camps of the like-minded—liberals and conservatives, secularists and religionists, to name just a few. We find great comfort in being right and in having company in being right. Religionists insist on the rightness of the world they imagine by sometimes proudly denouncing secular science and progressive thinking by pointing to the secular assumption that we can and should accept any and all claims of science and any and all forms of tolerance. There is no doubt that these are real assumptions, but in so doing they often fail to acknowledge, for example, their own dependence on science and to articulate and stand up for how their own religious traditions teach concern for the vulnerable and marginalized and charity and forbearance for all. Secularists strive to be good world-makers by avoiding delusions of transcendence, supernatural power or knowledge, and ideologies of convenience. They like to point to the dangerous religious tendency to identify God with one's own disposition, cultural circumstance, and ideology, which they remind us can bring to pass all kinds of immorality in the name of Deity. All of this is true, of course, but secularists never bother to explain how they avoid the same problem or how they will be capable of recognizing or recovering from their own occasional lousy conjecture about the world.

Since it is the nature of our minds to make worlds, we are also in the business of being creators and implicitly if not explicitly articulating our conception of what makes the world what it is. This is one reason why it seems to me that we can't escape the question of the nature of God, since we are either playing one or believing in one, or as the case may be, inescapably doing both. At its root the human condition seems to be a battle to identify sources of true transcendence so that somehow we can find a way out of the worlds we make and into a reality that proves to exist beyond our limitations or expectations, something we can believe in and work toward. The goal is to then be able to transform ourselves and the world we live in into something far better. Our moral challenge, in other words, is to be capable, despite the limitations of even the most well-conceived worlds we might make, of recognizing and embracing truth, even if or especially when it challenges our worldview or moves us to change. What I love about Latter-day Saint Christianity is that it recognizes the dangers of our world-making powers, admits to the inevitability of bad poetry even in the highest levels of accomplishment (think of how many times the Lord chastises Joseph Smith), and yet welcomes the best our imaginations can come up with as necessary tools to building God's kingdom and honors the inspired results (think of the brother of Jared and his request for the illuminated stones). The restored gospel of The Church of Jesus Christ of Latter-day Saints is the dream of transforming weaknesses into strengths—or bringing our will into harmony with God—and finding ourselves both making and made, human and divine, a process beautifully described in Moroni 7. The only reason to hope that the world we have imagined can harmonize with the world God reveals is the promise of God's atoning power.

This, I believe, requires submission to possibility—the possibility that I am wrong about the world, the possibility that I can be instructed through revelation from a divine power and that I and the world around me can change. I, for one, cannot separate the meaning of such submission from the idea of submitting to God. To believe that I can change the world, in other words, cannot be separated from the need to believe that I can and must change myself, that I can, even if only momentarily, transcend myself and even transcend the world I imagine myself to be in. As much as we might want to admire those who aspire to self-transcendence just by the sheer power of their will or through education alone, in the end it makes little sense to preclude the possibility that we need or might have access to power and insight beyond our natural capacities.

My own faith in such power has been strengthened by real, even if small, change I have observed in myself when I have tried to submit my will to God's. Small and personal change bolsters my hope that larger-scale change in society is possible. It is, of course, heartbreaking to have to admit to oneself that change is sometimes illusory, that we prematurely or impatiently declared victory before we collapsed back into our old self. But it is also God's atoning gift to sustain us in hope so as to continue in the effort after such disillusionments. Forbearing and patient love is required for the fact that our personality, for better and for worse, has been shaped by genes, history, and culture. It is one thing to see ourselves as products of our time. This is much of what education starts to reveal to us. But it is another thing altogether to move forward in hope after such a realization instead of collapsing into disillusionment and despair. Such hope does not come naturally or by will but as a gift from God, a gift we finally ask for when we discover the limits of the will. This then becomes the same patience and hope with which we can enter a world we are determined to change.

I am not saying that we should wait to change or even perfect ourselves before we should try to change the world. We cut our teeth in such attempts to better the world. And besides, we could end up waiting too long. But if we put the cart of societal change ahead of the horse of personal submission to God, we risk having no mechanism by which to double-check our judgments of others and of society and measure them against our own vanity, insecurities, unresolved conflicts, or biases. In other words, we might not have anything to stop us from creating an image of the ideal world after our own image, a world that sustains rather than challenges our most basic instincts and desires, the very instincts and desires we expected others to rise above.

Some people live in nirvanas of their own making, others in a hell of their own imagining. I like to think we are answerable for the worlds we choose to believe are real. And the best test of the worth of such worlds is how generously they illuminate potential *and* actual goodness in others *and* in ourselves.

It is fair and important to look at the institutional church and ask, "Are the cultural aspects of our particular Latter-day Saint moment the sum total of what the church or the gospel is? Is this all the institution is capable of? Has it made its full usefulness to the world evident?" And clearly the answer has to be no. This is not a heretical thing to say. Quite the contrary. It is akin to asking, "Is my idea or understanding of God sufficient to sum up who or what God is?" Of course not. But disbeliev-

> I don't believe it is possible to stay
> in the church and move it toward what
> it is striving to become if we can't properly
> recognize what it is already doing or
> has already done well.

ers like to jump on such inadequacies of belief as evidence of the folly of faith when in fact the inadequacy of belief is already something Christianity openly acknowledges. Precisely because it is inadequate and insufficient, we call it faith and not merely belief or conviction. We hope it can become more than it is, and we recognize the distance between the actuality and the potentiality of belief even if we can't measure it exactly. And why can't we measure it? For one, we can't know the actuality of belief—that is, we can't know what belief is doing in actual practice—without sufficient hindsight. And for another, we can't know without sufficient time where belief will take us. If this sounds like an impossible bind, it is only to say that we cannot escape questions of faith. Whatever our hope, whatever our philosophy, and whatever our drive and motivations, they are based on principles of faith, and only through experimentation—the sufficient suspension of disbelief—will the value of such principles be made manifest.

So to be aware of a gap between what the church is and what it might yet become should be a position of hope, not despair, a trust in process and movement toward something greater. That is not to say we are wrong to point out what we perceive to be its failings. It is only to say we haven't finished the work of hope for a better world just by pointing out institutional or cultural or political failings of a given institution or moment in our society, least of all if our own self-reformation is not our first priority. The scramble I described earlier to avoid being deceived has led perhaps to the ultimate deception: that we have secured our rightness by keeping our focus exclusively on the hypocrisies of institutions. Have you noticed the predominance today of the fetishized narratives about the failings of government, as if pointing out such failings guaranteed anything at all about the individual fortunate enough to have noticed them? And if you yourself feel that these narratives are overblown and hopeless, it is because you see the good that government still does and because you feel an investment, even a moral responsibility, to continue to do the hard effort of making democracy work. If you are an engaged citizen, it is because you know those failings intimately, not because you are blind to them. You are engaged precisely because you see them and because you have hope in overcoming them.

There is no question that such fetishizing is enabled not by more accurate knowledge of government conspiracies, as the critics pretend, but because of more selfish disengagement and a loss of hope. Is this any different from the fetishized narratives about the failings of the church promoted by its critics in and out of the church? Many of those who tire of or bristle at these narratives do so because they already have their sleeves rolled up and are at work to make the kingdom of God a reality. It feels like an insult to their best efforts. They aren't naive about the failings of the church. How could they be if they have spent any time working hard to provide a satisfactory and spiritually healthy environment for members? Indeed, the fact of their involvement makes them *part of those failings.* That's the inherent risk you take if you want to be part of the solution. No one gets off, you see, but least of all those who disengage entirely and imagine themselves innocent in their like-minded bubbles of cynicism.

The question, then, becomes whether or not we are willing to take the moral risk of seeing an institution through to realize its potential. I don't believe it is possible to stay in the church and move it toward what it is striving to become if we can't properly recognize what it is already doing or has already done well. I don't write this as a mere defensiveness on behalf of church leadership, just for its own sake. I don't doubt that religion, poorly used, has a dangerous tendency to create a culture of apathy that always accepts the status quo, but I don't believe that the fault for this lies at the feet of Christ or his church. It has something instead to do with our own relationship to God's word. The word of God is a mirror, says James, and we see an image of ourselves in it that should provide a roadmap for radical self-transformation, but that will depend on us, on whether we will take the word seriously enough to be moved to action, to change, so that we know ourselves more deeply, more clearly, and so that hopefully we come to know ourselves as Christians, God's spiritually begotten sons and daughters (see James 1:23; Moroni 7). If we are unwilling to use religion as a method for self-criticism and self-reformation, as James warns, then when we look into the mirror of our ideals and believe we see a complete reflection of ourselves as fully realized, we go happily on our way, believing erroneously that we are doing just fine. It is well known by most thinkers and dreamers that it is far easier to think well than to act well, especially when we compare the ease and excitement with which we are drawn to noble, high ideals and the almost indecipherable and impenetrable morass of institutional, cultural, and personal complexity that presents such discouraging prospects for change. So this transformation is not merely a matter of having the right ideals; it is a matter of whether or not we are willing to access sufficient power that will enable this transformation. As I said before, I believe this is God's power. I suspect that the failure to access it and instead forge it on our own has caused no small amount of suffering and injustice in the world. Simply put, it is more important to be engaged in the work of becoming good than to expend our energy insisting that we are already right. This is a lesson believers have yet to master.

I am certainly convinced, by the way, that the gospel does not see individual and societal transformation as separate processes or goals, despite our tendency to pursue the former at the expense of the latter. The only caveat seems to be that the gospel, at least in the age of globalization after Christ, is not a political but a transcultural moral philosophy chiefly, leaving the details of how to build civilization up to us as citizens of various cultures, nations, and regions. If it must be the case that society will always fall short of gospel principles, this happens no more or less frequently than we fall short as individuals. Revelation 2:26–27 in the Joseph Smith Translation, as just one example, states that "to him who overcometh, and keepeth my commandments unto the end, will I give power over many kingdoms." Here these verses make the explicit connection between personal obedience to the word and the transformation into a society governed not so much by law or tradition but by "faith, with equity and justice." The verses hint that this can be in this life, but it may also be promised for the next. Perhaps this could be said of all religions, but Christianity, in particular, is quite adept at recognizing the fundamental flaws of human nature that would make belief in religion a dangerous thing. We might wish either the teachings of the gospel or human tendencies to be otherwise, but we might not spend our energy wisely by trying to reinvent human tendencies or to reinvent the gospel. I prefer to go as deeply as I can within the teachings of Christ to find reasons for hope, grounds for change, and a call to higher morality.

Apathy in religious communities about world problems—about materialism and greed, about poverty, war, and human suffering, or about environmental degradation, to name a few—is perhaps the most disappointing discovery for anyone who expects religion to be relevant to our circumstances. Perhaps you can see how this disappointing tendency in religious communities is a function of the same problem we were describing earlier. These are messy, sometimes intractable problems, and to roll up our sleeves to try to do something about them might mean we are more able to see how we are part of the problems when we had preferred to believe that we could stay above the fray. When such collective apathy or ignorance about what troubles the world is pervasive and uncriticized, calls for institutional loyalty can be especially disappointing. Don't ever let yourself believe that being a Latter-day Saint means choosing an identity that excludes concerns about the world, no matter how others have fashioned their Latter-day Saint identity around such apathy. Such members have likely fallen victim to a reassurance and comfort that allows them to feel they can afford to take as their own the airline motto "Sit back, relax, and enjoy the flight!" Take comfort in the Lord's call to be anxiously engaged in a good cause (Doctrine and Covenants 58:27). Look on those not so engaged with pity and compassion. Help them imagine a new world, to discover the true wells of faith and charity in their tradition that will make them adequate to the problems we face. If you do, you will perhaps do more to help your religious tradition realize its potential than in any other way. I say let the world be filled with young Latter-day Saints who are known for their determination

Political and cultural apathy notwithstanding, there is very little doctrinal reason for any of us to hesitate in pursuing our political, social, and cultural dreams as members of the church.

to fight human and sex trafficking, racism and sexism, abuse and torture, environmental degradation, poverty and inequality, and war not despite but because of their Latter-day Saint faith.

Apathy cannot thrive without reinforcement, and such reinforcement is collective. That seems fundamental to group dynamics. But great good is also collective and must be collectively achieved. What stands in opposition to such apathy are principles, beliefs, and practices that are all central to the institutional church. So if these beliefs and practices are not producing a sufficient moral response to the world we live in, if believers simply are not witnessing sufficiently the profound moral principles of their own religion, the fault lies as much or more with them than it does with the institution. Because of the tendency of bureaucratization and a deep survival instinct, institutions often become obstacles to their own best intentions, but what also saves them are those who stay loyal to its highest principles. In other words, it isn't as if the institution in all of its historical and collective wisdom, including, of course, the teachings of the prophets, does not already contain the very remedies that the religious community seems to need. Western culture has produced monstrosities of hypocrisy, but it has also produced its own best criticisms, and historical Christianity and even our corner of the restored gospel are no different. The constituent elements of society's conscience are there in our writers, poets, prophets, scriptures, artists, and even some good civic leaders. I have never heard any leader of the church preach indifference, although I have no doubt that the worldviews of individual church leaders have never been completely sufficient. Their prophetic power lies more in their capacity to remind us of the need for hope in Christ in our times than it does in offering a comprehensive guide to the world's problems and their root causes. And hope in Christ certainly means, among other things, finding the faith to believe that we are called, in our small but important way, to make a difference in the world. This requires overcoming the force of all the many small and frequent ways we reinforce apathy and inaction in our collective culture. Political and cultural apathy and blank stares in church meetings notwithstanding, there is very little doctrinal reason for any of us to hesitate in pursuing our political, social, and cultural dreams as members of the church. The only reasons for our hesitation, in my view, are cultural. We don't like to stick out. We don't want to be suspected of having an agenda. But if we make it clear that our motivations are grounded in making Christ, his gospel, and his church the central cornerstone of the effort, I think we are on solid footing.

If it isn't obvious by now, what I am suggesting is that departing from an institution in the name of principles it wholly subscribes to but insufficiently lives up to does not help it realize its potential. The temptation, for some, is to believe, falsely in my opinion, that the ideals of the gospel are opposed to the secular wisdom of our day. There have been, of course, moments of real tension between the church and the world, as there always will be, but seeing their differences as inevitable and irreconcilable is to see both the gospel and, for example, human rights penuriously and not as different expressions of similar values. The church needs more members, not fewer, who honor and preach and live to realize the most ambitious and far-reaching implications of its beliefs. I believe this is what Richard Bushman meant when he called for a "radiant Mormonism."[2] Of course, given the weight of collective apathy and collective acceptance of the status quo, this means such individual members must have rare courage, deep confidence and trust in their own understandings of spiritual truth, and unquestionable integrity. And they must learn the patience to work to persuade others that their individual convictions have collective relevance. If it is true that revelations from God through his prophets still require ratification among believers over time to obtain their greatest potency as truth, it is likely also true that obscure and marginalized voices, no matter the virtue of their individual convictions, require the rhetorical power of persuasion and the sustaining and persistent force of charity to move from the margin to the center and to realize their full potential. It is the very marrow of religious faith to do this necessary work to bring the obscure to light; to integrate into, rather than to marginalize oneself from, the institution; to teach and to be taught.

---

2. Richard Bushman, "Richard Bushman: Embracing a 'Radiant' Mormonism," *Deseret News*, November 16, 2017.

When faced with the extremism of Pharisees, I know it is common to insist that love is more important than obedience and that the spirit is more important than the letter, but it is unfortunate that such positions so often result in a lax attitude about taking commandments seriously. As opposed as he was to fanatics, Christ never preached love at the expense of obedience. As Alma warned, we are never to excuse ourselves and deny the justice of God, and this is because this also denies his mercy (see Alma 42:30). In my experience, sometimes the spirit of the law requires more intense conformity to the law than we thought. For example, Christ said it was not enough to avoid adultery but to also avoid adulterous thoughts (see Matthew 5:27–28). We don't have the ears to hear this sometimes. Some obey without love, for its own sake, and they use coercion and intimidation to inspire obedience and consequently fail to do good in their obedience. Others naturally gravitate to the good feelings of love but fail to do the work to empower it to its fullest capacity through the grace that comes from more complete submission to God's will. This is what Paul is getting at in his famous discourse about charity (see 1 Corinthians 13). Without God's love and grace to bless and sanctify our actions, we are nothing. I am not suggesting that we "earn" this grace through obedience, but it is folly to allow the fanaticism of others, their lack of love, or their apathy about world problems as an excuse to avoid trying with all of our might, mind, and strength to do what he asks.

I do wish we Latter-day Saints would learn that morality includes far more than a morality of the body, and I certainly don't find the political status quo in church culture acceptable, but I am afraid that there isn't an easy solution to these problems. Are we too materialistic? Yes. Are we sometimes guilty of nationalism? Of course. Are we ignorant of environmental degradation? All too often. Has sexism been used to justify the priesthood structure of the church? A no-brainer. I could go on.

But if we assume that wholesale institutional corruption is the root of the problem, then we must believe that wholesale revolution is the only answer and we must assume that the ideals that motivate us somehow have nothing to do with fundamental Christian ideals. In my experience, such categorical conclusions about the church, about an institution like a university or a business, or even about the state or federal governments are the result of poor thinking and are often motivated by a desire to escape the burdens of uncertainty, personal responsibility, and the complexity of human beings. We want diagnoses that are clear and unambiguous and that don't implicate ourselves. I recently read these words from Wendell Berry:

> The question, What can we do? especially when the problem is large, implies the expectation of a large solution.
>
> I have no solution to offer. There is, as maybe we all have noticed, a conspicuous shortage of large-scale corrections for problems that have large-scale causes. . . . The aftermath of a bombing has to be dealt with one corpse, one wound at a time. And so the first temptation to avoid is the call for some sort of revolution. To imagine that destructive power might be made harmless by gathering enough power to destroy it is of course perfectly futile. . . . Arrogance cannot be cured by greater arrogance, or ignorance by greater ignorance. To counter the ignorant use of knowledge and power we have, I am afraid, only a proper humility.[3]

In another passage, I read these burning words:

> Mere opposition finally blinds us to the good of the things we are trying to save. And it divides us hopelessly from our opponents, who no doubt are caricaturing us while we are demonizing them.

---

3.   Wendell Berry, *The Way of Ignorance: And Other Essays* (Berkeley, CA: Counterpoint, 2016), 62–63.

We lose, in short, the sense of shared humanity. . . . An effort that is defined only or mainly by a problem is negative necessarily.[4]

I am not accusing you or anyone else who is sincerely and deeply concerned about the welfare of society of being arrogant or blind or negative. I am merely pointing to the ethical challenges of resisting the problems we face. It seems we cannot expect more than partial success. This is no reason to stop caring or to stop trying. It is not the same thing as saying change is impossible, but if we believe that any logic advocating moderation or patience is only and always a betrayal, we may bypass the best tools in our midst we could have used and potential allies we could have summoned. Berry is giving us a cause for caution, patience beyond what would seem warranted, and peace in doing the little we can. I think he would agree that our ability to accept these limitations comes from Christ; it is, in Berry's words, the "burden of the Gospels" to "accept our failure to understand, not as a misstatement or a textual flaw or as a problem to be solved, but as a question to live with and a burden to be borne."[5]

There is, I know, something deeper and more personal at stake in these comments for you. And I tread on this ground with trepidation and a prayer in my heart that I will not come across as presumptuous or oblivious to your circumstances. I only know you in part, and I am eager to be corrected and enlightened about your spiritual life and struggles. My impression is that you are more deeply Christian, more indebted to the church and to the gospel, more suited to build the Lord's kingdom, more deeply doing the work of bringing the power of the atonement into many people's lives than perhaps you realize. But as much strength as others already draw from you, I believe they will draw even more strength if they see that you

---

4. Berry, *Way of Ignorance*, 74.
5. Berry, *Way of Ignorance*, 131.

are unambiguously clear about your fundamental submission to God and to Christ. I hope this doesn't sound like a judgment of your person. It is, rather, an advocacy of a certain kind that I want to encourage you to consider. If people can see that the terms of submission are those we all recognize in the church as the fundamentals, you and those who admire and are inspired by you will draw more strength from God than from you.

If we do not keep pointing people to God, to Christ, to a power higher than our own, and instead only point fingers of blame, we will fail. When our allusions to this power seem disconnected from or unrelated to the institution of the church, I fear we may weaken others in their capacity to access the potent and saving power of the atonement. If we can access the power to do those things that we are called to do to build the kingdom in the broadest sense, perhaps others will follow, but then it won't be about ideas or personalities but about God's power in human lives. And this is really the point. You and I have some good ideas—maybe even very good ones—about how to make a good society, or at least we might be able to argue what one should or could look like. But I think God in the end must be our guide in how to make this happen. Unless I learn the discipline that brings me into contact with that guidance, I will be working only for a purely self-made vision. If we go forward to do this unarmed by the power that comes from such submission to "every word that proceedeth out of the mouth of God" (Matthew 4:4), we may end up creating a god and a vision of justice merely after our own image. This god we have invented might be a relatively nice one, a moral one on the whole, and politically very cool, but he might not be the real One, the One who endows us with real power to make the world as *He* would design it. We will work alone for a cause that can be achieved only with divine help and one that we have ill-defined because of *mortal*, if not moral, shortsightedness.

Church Life and the Discipline of Renewal

R ecently I had a dream about a quest for deeper conversion, and in it I was pushing myself along a series of unending, unconnected, and half-broken railroad tracks with no end in sight. I awoke disturbed, trying to decipher its meaning. Was I trapped in a maze of bureaucracy? Was I engaged in a labor that took me to no place in particular? So many meetings, so many responsibilities, so many reasons to feel guilty and enervated. It raised the question for me: where can I turn for renewal when even the religion I have chosen and have faith in stops providing me with the feelings of joy it once gave me?

It seems there is a paradox at the heart of the practice of religion. Religion is designed to produce rich experiences of spirituality both individually and in communities—experiences often characterized by their renewing power—but it relies on repetition, ritual, and habit in order to produce such results. My Latter-day Saint religion provides a variety of exercises to assist me in cultivating the discipline and practice of such spirituality. For example, I am encouraged to pray and read the scriptures daily, to attend church every Sunday for two hours, and to serve in a calling in my church community in order to help the community cohere and grow together. I am encouraged to attend the temple regularly, to minister to others, to do my family history work, to keep my body pure, and so on. It's a long list, and even though

> It isn't the outward practice that defines the meaning of our religion but what happens on the inside. And no one, not my religious leaders, not my parents, my wife, my role models, not even God, is responsible for my own heart.

I have come to depend on this structure of my church to assist me in my spiritual growth, like many members of the church, I suppose, there are times when it feels that the very structure of these practices gets in the way of my growth. Would one would be better off without so many rituals, so many practices?

But I wonder if that is the right question. Jesus said it isn't what goes in but what comes out of us that defiles us (see Matthew 15:11). It isn't the outward practice that defines the meaning of our religion but what happens on the inside. And no one, not my religious leaders, not my parents, my wife, my role models, not even God, is responsible for my own heart. Besides, the problem is that, at least in my experience, every time I have drifted in my habits and discipline of church life, I generally have found poorer results. Maybe at first there is a feeling of release, a kind of lightening of the burden and the illusion of freedom. But generally the go-it-alone approach for me starts to promote a greater self-ishness, and distraction and greed and arrogance take the place of focus, modesty, and humility, and I place my relationships and myself in harm's way. There are, of course, very real reasons, grounded in the behavior of others, for which some people find church a toxic place to be. But in my personal experience, intentional wandering from what I believe to be God's law inhibits the spiritual growth I seek. I rely on my own conscience and my own will, as I should, but part of that self-reliance includes an awareness of my potential for self-deception and therefore the need for communal gathering.

Besides, as challenging as it can sometimes be to have to work within the context of a community to whom I am somehow answerable, I am better as a member of a community than I am by myself. I can't account for all the ways my association with my fellow Saints has blessed my life. Because my weaknesses inspire me to remain close to the community of Christ and to lean on the Savior himself, I am grateful for them. I am better when I strive to be my brother's keeper and to maintain a commitment to do whatever service is asked of me. When I take the gospel seriously and serve others even if initially only out of duty, I find I like the person I am becoming.

To be perpetually renewed by a lifelong commitment to praxis is a little like the challenge of keeping the fire and passion of romantic love alive in a marriage as it moves into its second, third, and fourth decade. How can a relationship feel new when, precisely because of our attachment to what it makes us feel, it has become so familiar that we almost lose feeling altogether? How can we stir the old feelings, even renew them altogether, without deviating from our commitments? How can we avoid being satisfied with a staid and habitual spirituality, which is really no spirituality at all?

I believe one often-overlooked tool is language, which when properly used, can help open our eyes to ignored or unseen sources of richness and renewal in religious life. We often fail to honor the mystery and depth of what we experience in life by resorting to familiar clichés, tired metaphors, and formulaic expressions. We do this almost unconsciously. Because religious communities practice together, it is so easy to form habits of speech that work for everyone. We pass on phrases to one another, like the favorite dinnertime prayer phrase "to nourish and strengthen," which in my family line is at least four generations old. We talk of "feeling the Spirit" or "losing the Spirit," and we talk of gaining an "eternal perspective" and "applying the atonement" and being "impressed" to do or say something. Even doctrinally prescribed language can cause us to grow lazy in our thinking, as if we all already know what such terms as "the spirit of Elijah" might mean or what it means to call each other "brother" and "sister" or to "partake" of the sacrament and "always remember" Christ. There is nothing inherently wrong with such words and phrases. But when we take in the whole of our lives and our experiences as a religious people, we begin to see how superficially we have treated things and how inadequate words can be to describe the deepest levels of experience.

Language works best when it helps us see or at least imagine more than what it signifies, rather than less, which is to say that we ought to be more careful about the language we use to describe sacred things.

It helps to recognize the inherent weakness of language and our limitations as language users. I think we are on the right track if we find ourselves almost incapable of describing what it is we experience and feel instead of allowing language to become reductive and habitual. To believe we have said enough or said it right is to fail to understand the inherent limitations of language and the inherent richness of spiritual things. We want to keep things simple. We should. But we shouldn't pretend that the gospel or life experiences or how we feel are ever simplistic. I am more and more amazed at how little I understand what we sometimes call "the workings of the Spirit," by which we mean the ways in which God strives to communicate to us and Christ's forgiving and healing love touches us. I like President Dieter F. Uchtdorf's caution that the atonement is the very heart of the most sacred dimensions of our experience and that for this reason we ought to be careful not to speak of it too lightly.[1] Let us not trivialize that which is sacred by rendering it simplistically. If we truly mean to encompass all its meanings, we must confess that "workings of the Spirit" seeks to capture not only "impressions" or answers to our prayers but also our dreams, our intuitions, unspoken feelings, the comings and goings of past memories, events that take years to interpret their meaning, even the long journey of human history. Life itself is a long dialogue with God. It may be interrupted by our distractions, blurred by our confusions, and stifled by our arrogance, but life can be marked as a series of returns to that deep place within our soul where things are still and where love abounds. When we find ourselves in that place within us, whether we arrive there by intention, serendipity, or grace, we wonder why we ever left.

I have found that the power of poetry has helped me perceive and experience the mysteries of life and of God more profoundly. I especially enjoy poets like Rainer Maria Rilke, Pablo Neruda, W. B. Yeats, Mary Oliver, Walt Whitman, and T. S. Eliot, but there are many, many others who help give me a different vocabulary for experience. I enjoy the prose of Marilynne Robinson, Toni Morrison, Wallace Stegner, Virginia Woolf, Herman Melville, and many others for the same reason. The central ambition of the literary arts is to take up the rudiments

---

1.   Dieter F. Uchtdorf, "The Gift of Grace," *Ensign*, May 2015, 107.

of ordinary language and experience and create a new world of possibility. The power of the technology we know as language is that instead of obsessively needing yet another fantastical rendering of reality, facilitated by digital enhancements or willful distortions of normality, poetry gives itself the same challenge religion provides—how to find awe and wonder in the face of what we see every day. Take, for example, this beautiful passage from a Derek Walcott poem, a man who for over seventy years never failed to identify surprising beauty on his small island of St. Lucia. Nearing the end of his life, he wrote:

> There are the days when every street corner rounds itself into a sunlit surprise, a painting or a phrase, canoes drawn up by the market, the harbour's blue, the barracks. So much to do still, all of it praise.[2]

What kind of eyes does it take to see the most ordinary and familiar reality as a "sunlit surprise"? What a joy to be able to see each day in our own familiar neck of the woods as a gift, worthy of our praise!

I am surprised that reading great writers from all walks of life is not a more regular practice among us as Latter-day Saints. We serve, but we also do a lot of talking to and with each other in church, so it matters that we wield language well. I suspect that reading great literature would do a great deal to widen our vicarious experience and energize, revive, and stimulate our vocabulary so that we could more adequately meet the challenges of existence. If we fail to read great writers and instead rely increasingly on journalistic prose or, worse, the daily communications of texting and social media, we will never know or

---

2. Derek Walcott, *White Egrets: Poems* (New York: Farrar, Straus, and Giroux, 2011), 82 (poem no. 51).

appreciate the tools that are available to us. This results in circulating the same language in a world of clichés. We aren't clichés. Our lives are rich, but if clichés are the only lenses through which we perceive reality, we can scarcely claim to perceive it at all. Seeing the world through different (and especially gifted) eyes allows the truthfulness and universality of experience to stand out even more clearly. One catches from their pens words and phrases that drop into one's hands as gifts to aid in the quest for deeper self-understanding. I have found that reading and listening to writers of faith talk about their experiences is similarly rich. I have especially enjoyed reading Marilynne Robinson, C. S. Lewis, and Thomas Merton. I love working with people of other faiths on a common cause. I never tire of talking to people

> In tragedy, a person's wrongdoing brings consequences that are disproportionate to the action, and, indeed, much of our suffering is the result of this very pattern. And Christ's disproportionate grace is the answer.

who see the world differently. Such conversations make me more careful and thoughtful about how I think about my own experience. I recently listened to an interview Krista Tippett did with John O'Donohue, and I found myself inspired at every turn by his capacity to give expression to things I had experienced but for which I had up to that point found (and maybe thoughtlessly borrowed) words only from the ever-available storehouse of clichés.[3]

Another example: I recently read the *Oxford Study Bible*, my first thorough venture through the Bible in another translation, and I saw and experienced the book as if for the first time. This is not to say that the King James Bible isn't beautiful in its own right. It is regal, sumptuous, and close to my heart, but precisely because it is so well known to me, a little defamiliarization helped open up new terrain. In the KJV we read, for example, "For if through the offence of one many be dead, much more the grace of God, and the gift by grace, which is by one man, Jesus Christ, hath abounded unto many" (Romans 5:15). In the *Oxford Study Bible*, however, we read, "But God's act of grace is out of all proportion to Adam's wrongdoing. For if the wrongdoing of that one man brought death upon so many, its effect is vastly exceeded by the grace of God and the gift that came by the grace of God and the gift that came to so many by the grace of the one man, Jesus Christ." One could argue over which is a more faithful translation, but what jumped out to my mind reading the *Oxford Study Bible* was that Christ was the answer to the riddle of tragedy. In tragedy a person's wrongdoing brings consequences that are disproportionate to the action, and, indeed, much of our suffering is the result of this very pattern. And Christ's disproportionate grace is the answer. I could have scarcely seen this idea in the KJV alone.

I not only have learned from different translations, but in the humanities, I have discovered many retellings and adaptations of biblical stories as well as entirely new narratives inspired by the Bible. Whenever I revisit an old story that has been reframed entirely—as I did, for example, after reading the story of Cain

---

3.   John O'Donohue, interview by Krista Tippett, *On Being*, August 6, 2015, https://onbeing.org/programs/john-odonohue-the-inner-landscape -of-beauty-aug2017/.

and Abel in John Steinbeck's *East of Eden* or after watching Darren Aronofsky's use of Jewish midrash in his film *Noah* or after listening to Bach's *Christmas Oratorio* or after viewing Rembrandt's depiction of Abraham's attempted sacrifice of Isaac—I have felt as if I never really paid close enough attention to the original story. And I have made an earnest commitment to never treat the familiar quite so shallowly again. I have found myself returning to read the old story with a renewed hope to hear the strains of what is yet to be, what is missing between the words, and what I can do to allow language to say more than it does. That is, after all, how I read when I first fell in love with scripture and what I need to feel from time to time lest the endless repetition of scripture study and the repetitions of religious life become a fruitless exercise. Avoid vain repetitions, Christ said, but pray always (see Matthew 6:7; Luke 18:1). That's enough of a challenge right there to keep me busy for the rest of my life. I want to be like the artists who generate new thoughts, new words, new questions, new pleas all while recurring to the same texts, the same structure, the same commitments.

I know I am often sloppy with language and careless at prayer, and as a result I am blind to much of experience. As a result, I might miss seeing God's glory in this world and appreciating what is most sacred and meaningful. There are so many beautiful words and so many marvelous ways to dialogue with God. Silence can still speak, of course, and it often speaks more than words, so renewal isn't always merely a matter of finding better words to honor experience. Honoring holiness might also involve the wisdom to know when the truth of experience requires me to say nothing at all.

John O'Donohue wrote, "It's strange to be here. The mystery never leaves you." Krista Tippet asked him what he meant, and this was his answer: "Thought is the face that we put on the meaning that we feel and that we struggle with, and that the world is always larger and more intense and stranger than our best thought will ever reach."[4] To understand that thought itself is secondary to the experience we have with others is to understand more clearly the mystery of another human face. And to do this we can draw on the Christian concept of *imago dei*—the biblical teaching that reminds us that we are all created in the image of God and are therefore all, each in our own way, various manifestations of his presence. An encounter with another, then, is a holy encounter, one that requires our utmost reverence. Marilynne Robinson reminds us that habit, or more specifically the habit of modern secularism and its particularly insidious manifestation as consumerism, causes us to look at others and judge them quickly for their immediate use to us, rather than face the wonder and miracle of our mutual existence. As Robinson warns, we are in danger of objectifying the soul— our own and those of others—and "measur[ing] creation's worth on conditional terms rather than on the merit of being created and sustained by a mindful creator."[5] It seems that if we saw ourselves as creatures, as dependent children created out of love and mercy and interdependent on one another, it would be hard to justify any act that objectifies, demeans, or ignores the humanity of others. We would, instead, be filled with the wonder of being itself. If we knew a sacrament meeting was going to be our last supper with one another, how differently would we see it? As a result of reading a great deal of Rilke and watching the wonderful film *Wings of Desire*, I sometimes find myself imagining how I will miss what I am experiencing after I am dead, and this helps keep me ever more alive.

---

4.   John O'Donohue interview.

5.   Marilynne Robinson, *The Givenness of Things: Essays* (New York: Farrar, Straus, and Giroux, 2015), 113.

"Being at church" can mean attendance, but I want to think about the "wonder of being" that might happen at church. The mystery and wonder of discovering the individual reality and life story of other people could be enough to keep us engaged at church. No matter how homogenous a ward might at first appear, if it is filled with individuals, it is filled with diversity, wonder, and beautiful strangeness. The only reason it doesn't seem that way, it seems to me, is because we haven't done the work nor exercised the imagination enough to begin to perceive the outlines of the many and diverse stories around us. We ought to be, as the novelist Henry James once said of novelists, the kind of person on whom nothing is lost.[6] And we cannot truly discover others without striving to serve them, and to truly discover another is to rediscover ourselves, so it is safe to say that the burden is on us to be curious enough to allow church to provide endless opportunity for renewal. This is especially the case because we are bound together by Christ's invitation to come unto him. When things get stale or when I feel alienated, I have found that it helps to pay attention to others with more charity for and more interest in their life stories. In 2 Nephi 26:33 we read: "He inviteth them all to come unto him and partake of his goodness; and he denieth none that come unto him, black and white, bond and free, male and female; and he remembereth the heathen; and all are alike unto God, both Jew and Gentile." We could say that the central message of the Book of Mormon is that there will be one fold and one shepherd, that all differences and conflicts throughout history will become a meaningful part of the great gathering in the last days. This is a tremendous challenge, but it is exciting and renewing work to strive to create more unity and a more welcoming spirit in church and to learn to see the likeness of

---

6. See Henry James, "The Art of Fiction," *Longman's Magazine*, September 4, 1884.

God in each person I meet. We can think of other people as our opportunity rather than as our challenge to find new meaning and value in church service if we have the willingness to learn their stories. This happens through deepening bonds of friendship as we listen more attentively to one another and are willing to truly adopt one another as brothers and sisters.

Jesus recited the entirety of chapter 54 of Isaiah when he met with the Nephites. In other words, it was an exact repetition. But note how powerfully this makes these words come alive and highlights the importance of making new family bonds with strangers. It begins: "Sing, O barren, thou that didst not bear; break

---

We have a special responsibility to make enough room in our homes, in our wards, and in our hearts so that even though we are a small minority, we could, if asked, bring the whole world into the fold of God.

---

forth into singing, and cry aloud, thou that didst not travail with child; for more are the children of the desolate than the children of the married wife, saith the Lord." And then these powerful words: "Enlarge the place of thy tent, and let them stretch forth the curtains of thine habitations; spare not, lengthen thy cords and strengthen thy stakes" (3 Nephi 22:1–2).

At least one interpretation of this is that there are more people who do not enjoy the strength of a stable family life than those who do, and even fewer who enjoy the covenants of the restored gospel. This casts the experience of going to church in an entirely different light. We come because although we all come from biological families of all kinds, we seek surrogate relationships. We seek the compensation of friendship and spiritual brother- and sisterhood to achieve a deeper sense of belonging. This places a special responsibility on our shoulders to make enough room in our homes, in our wards, and in our hearts so that even though we are a small minority, we could, if asked, bring the whole world into the fold of God. Indeed, this is precisely what God has asked of us! This is a humbling mission, to say the least, but at least it means we should never get bored.

For this reason Joseph Smith spoke of the revolutionary power of friendship: "Friendship is one of the grand fundamental principles of 'Mormonism'; [it is designed] to revolutionize and civilize the world, and cause wars and contentions to cease and men to become friends and brothers. . . . It unites the human family with its happy influence."[7] President Howard W. Hunter also said: "We need a more peaceful world, growing out of more peaceful families and neighborhoods and communities. To secure and cultivate such peace, as the Prophet Joseph Smith taught us, 'we must love others, even our enemies as well as our friends.' . . . We need to extend the hand of friendship. We need to be kinder, more gentle, more forgiving, and slower to anger."[8] More friendship and deeper friendship is how we enlarge our tent.

It seems unlikely that we can solve poverty, war, or ethnic conflict in an increasingly diverse nation and church if we are not truly inclusive and embracing of all our brothers and sisters within the immediate reach of our influence and do not look around and be more observant of those who fall by the wayside,

---

7. *History of the Church*, 5:517; from a discourse given by Joseph Smith on July 23, 1843, in Nauvoo, Illinois; reported by Willard Richards.
8. Howard W. Hunter, *That We Might Have Joy* (Salt Lake City: Deseret Book, 1994), 174.

who struggle to fit in, and who are tempted to leave. As Paul tells us, no one should feel like a stranger or a foreigner in the household of God (see Ephesians 2:19).

As strong as our community can sometimes be, we can be better friends and can help more people feel they truly belong. Without obvious common ground with others, our unique path in life can sometimes cause a feeling of isolation. President Uchtdorf assures us that if we knew each other better, we would see we had more in common. But he also suggests that we ought to think of differences as gifts to give to others instead of as barriers to friendship in the gospel: "Your background or upbringing might seem different from what you perceive in many Latter-day Saints, *but that could be a blessing.* Brothers and sisters, dear friends, we need your unique talents and perspectives. *The diversity of persons and peoples all around the globe is a strength of this Church.*"[9]

My brother's suicide when I was eighteen was shocking, and for many years I had a very difficult time sharing it with others. I doubted anyone would have any idea how it felt, and, to be honest, many didn't. Sometimes I heard others' testimonies and found myself resenting what felt like the ease of their faith. A few years later my other brother came out to me as gay. At first he didn't want me to share the information with anyone, and I think our family felt even more different and unsure if our story matched anyone else's. But as I got older and learned more about the suffering and unique circumstances of other people and their trials, and as I became more aware of individual gay and lesbian members of the church, I became more comfortable sharing my family story and made more friends as a result. I don't mean to sound harsh in saying this, but I have looked back

---

9. Dieter F. Uchtdorf, "Come, Join with Us," *Ensign*, November 2013, 23; emphasis added.

at my earlier alienation and realized that it was a function of my own broad and sweeping judgments of people whom I simply had not taken the time or made the effort to get to know. It is risky to open one's heart and share one's life story, so when people do, they need at least one true friend who will meet them where they are and accept and love them fully. For them to feel they belong, at least one of those people needs to be someone in church. Nothing renews me faster than becoming that person for someone else. I look forward to church more when I feel that perhaps someone needs me there.

There are as many potential reasons to feel like strangers and foreigners as there are members of the church. Maybe it is because you are single or divorced or widowed, or you are black or of mixed race or Asian or Hispanic, or maybe you grew up speaking Spanish or French or Chinese, or you were abused when you were young or you lost a parent, a child, or a sibling. Or maybe you struggle with addiction or you have fought your way into the church after a long life of sin, or you continue to struggle even after previous attempts to repent, or you have struggled your entire church life with anger or depression. Or maybe you have been attracted to those of the same sex your whole life, or you are in a marriage that is not as fulfilling as you had hoped, or you are a victim of abusive or dishonest relationships. Maybe you find yourself doubting the church and some of its teachings, or you are liberal and find yourself surrounded by conservatives, or you are conservative and feel as if your values are decreasingly appreciated. Maybe as a woman you feel your voice is not valued, that you are judged for being professionally successful or for not working and staying at home with your children. Maybe you have failed to realize your professional dreams, or you struggle with your body image, or you suffer from chronic pain and illness, or your children have strayed, or you are the only member or active member in your family. Maybe you struggle to believe like others seem to believe, or you came home early from a mission or never served. You get the idea. I could eventually describe every single one of us, which tells me that these reasons to feel alienated are also exciting challenges and gifts that we can consecrate to the Lord to make belonging a possibility for everyone.

This requires that we learn to love our own lives, whatever the path we have been on, and appreciate how God has made our weaknesses strong, and we honor his love for us when we courageously and lovingly share our stories with others. To love our lives, like loving our families and wards, doesn't mean that we believe everything is perfect or that God wished everything upon us, but it does mean that we accept that through his suffering on the cross, Christ became acquainted with and bore our grief, and therefore he alone can transform weakness into strength and thereby help us see the silver linings of our story. By letting others into our lives and by showing interest in the stories of others, we do our part in building friendships with our fellow ward members and making more room in the fold of God. My message is simple: the fold is not a mold.

Although we do a lot of socializing, the church is not a social club. President Uchtdorf made this very clear: "The Church is not an automobile showroom" where we can show off, but a place of "repair, maintenance, and rehabilitation[.] We come to church not to hide our problems but to heal them."[10] Remember Paul's words about the body of Christ. Let us not be like the foot and question our belonging just because we aren't a hand. Or the ear that doubts it belongs because it isn't an eye. "God appointed each limb and organ to its own place in the body"; he gave "special honor to the humbler parts," Paul tells us, to those parts most likely to doubt their significance, "so that there might be no division in the body" (1 Corinthians 12:18–26, New English

---

10. Dieter F. Uchtdorf, "On Being Genuine," *Ensign*, May 2015, 83.

Translation). In other words, we cannot have one fold and one shepherd as long as we neglect those who feel they are in the minority or on the margins, for whatever reason. Maybe they have imagined their own alienation, but that doesn't mean it still doesn't need to be overcome.

There are a great number of very strong models of family life in the church, so many that such strength can unintentionally alienate or intimidate others, but that only happens when we mistakenly assume there is only one mold. Remember: "all

---

Others are far more likely to reveal themselves to us if we show in the way we speak and conduct ourselves to be the kind of people to whom others can safely entrust their life stories.

---

are alike unto God" (2 Nephi 26:33). Let us repeat this phrase to ourselves from time to time. The fold of God places no value whatsoever on body type or looks, on age, marital status, nationality, gender, political persuasion, educational background, or career and income. We cannot run the risk of judging others. Elder Eyring taught: "When you meet someone, treat them as if they were in serious trouble, and you will be right more than half the time."[11] If someone is judgmental, it is tempting to make the same mistake and judge them. Nothing kills our chances for renewal more quickly than a spirit of unrighteous judgment.

---

11. Henry B. Eyring, "The Reward of Enduring Well," *Ensign*, July 2017, 14.

Judging others moves us away from the wonder of being and instead, as Marilynne Robinson explained, causes us to measure creation's worth as if it already wasn't infinitely valuable.[12] Judgment implies that right living, as important as it is to our happiness, creates our worth in the eyes of God. It confuses worthiness with worth.

And judgment begins with thoughts in the mind about our encounters with others and eventually finds its way into our language. Others are far more likely to reveal themselves to us if we show in the way we speak and conduct ourselves to be the kind of people to whom others can safely entrust their life stories. Standing up for what we believe should always be done in genuine love; it need not be occasion for fighting and contention. We are warned against behavior that would cause another to "esteem [us] to be [an] enemy" (Doctrine and Covenants 121:43). The bottom line is that to experience the wonder of being at church, our interactions need to go beyond the substance of Sunday School talk. Talk is cheap (including my own advice here). Talking about the gospel is not as important as living it. We must not make the mistake of believing that the point of life is to be right and expend our energy trying to correct people with words. The point of life is to be good, and over time, perhaps over decades, the quiet kindness and goodness and generosity of our lives will speak far more profoundly and loudly than any defense of the truth we will ever utter.

The purpose of the fold of God is to provide a refuge within the bonds of friendship so that we are inspired to make and keep sacred covenants, culminating in the covenants of the temple, that underwrite our chances for happiness in this life and guarantee happiness in the life to come. There is no room in God's fold for pressures to conform to norms that are out of reach,

---

12. Robinson, *Givenness of Things*, 113.

unfair, or arbitrary. But the gospel isn't just a call for tolerance for its own sake and a mere "live and let live" community. God gave us apostles and prophets "for the building up of the body of Christ, until we all attain to the unity inherent in our faith and in our knowledge of the Son of God" (Ephesians 4:12–13, New English Translation). So while our differences matter and are to be valued and we need to meet each other where we are, our differences are not essential to our identity; our goal is to use the atonement to build our true identity as Christ's sons and daughters and heirs of the kingdom.

Paul met people where they were. He befriended all. He spoke as a Greek to the Greeks and as a Jew to the Jews, but in the end his goal was something more profound than a big club of diverse people. His goal was the transformation of individuals into new creatures in Christ. He taught: "Be not conformed to this world: but be ye transformed by the renewing of your mind" (Romans 12:2). Transformation and renewal, in other words, are not facilitated so much by external circumstances as by an internal determination to accept Christ as our Savior and to covenant to remember him. Paul preached, "Baptized into union with him, you have all put on Christ like a garment. There is no such thing as Jew and Greek, slave and freeman, male and female; for you are all one person in Christ Jesus" (Galatians 3:27–28, New English Translation).

I believe in this transformative power of Christ's almighty atonement. I don't think it means that our Greek or Jewish or American or African American identities don't matter. It is lamentable that many today insist that the very act of speaking of differences divides us and should therefore stop. This might be a good point if it were true that all differences have been fairly recognized, but this is rarely the case, and least of all in situations where a strong majority is blind to the lived experiences of those on the margins. It is for this reason that Jesus called us to be like the good Samaritan—to befriend the friendless and to love our enemy. How can we obey this command if we don't even believe there are such categories of people? It is the height of arrogance for a majority culture to demand that minorities stop talking about their different lived experiences unless the majority is willing to acknowledge that their lived experiences are also different, and not universal as they have assumed. We cannot model Christian acceptance if we refuse to acknowledge, let alone honor, the lived experiences of others. It's true that our American culture is obsessed with identity and that, as a result, we have become very fractured. We probably need to learn to see beyond difference, but we can't see beyond difference meaningfully unless we learn to see difference in the first place. We can model ourselves after Paul and after Christ himself, who knows and honors all of our particularities but who also knows the differences between vital lived experiences that have shaped our differences to important and good ends and those superficial aspects of our identity that are probably less relevant to God's purposes, including our weaknesses. He sees us entirely and particularly, and yet he loves us perfectly.

For this reason we can say that Christ is the perfect friend. This is his church and kingdom we are trying to build, and his model of friendship that must guide us. I believe in the transformative power of true friendship in the gospel. I wouldn't be an active member today without many such friends who are my brothers and sisters in Christ. Their willingness to bear with me, to know me and love me, inspires me to go to church and offer the same sustaining hand to others. Exploring and deepening bonds of friendship in the gospel are what makes church life so fulfilling and life so full of wonder. When those relationships are alive, dynamic, and constantly growing, there are never enough words to describe how renewed I feel.

Waiting on the Lord, or Sustaining Church Leaders

There are many issues in the Church of Jesus Christ of Latter-day Saints today that are potentially divisive and challenging: LGBT rights, women and the priesthood, the history and current relevance of the practice of polygamy, the history of the priesthood and temple restriction, and others. Our conversations about these issues raise many questions. Does believing in prophets, seers, and revelators mean that we cannot ask questions about or even strongly disagree with policies, practices, or even doctrines and still be members in good standing? At what point should we question our own judgment instead? Does belief in revelation through prophets obligate us to believe that church leaders have never made mistakes *as* church leaders, that all of church history then is without blemish? If we admit to faults in the church's past, how do we show our faith and confidence in the present and in the future? Doesn't such faith and confidence include how we feel about ourselves and our own fallibility? In short, in a lay church like ours, what does it mean to sustain church leaders?

I don't pretend to have the definitive answers to these questions. Others have spoken wisely on these issues. I can speak only from my personal experience. Let me start by saying that I was raised to believe that I had a responsibility to use critical judgment with regard to church leaders. I was not raised on

> ## Faith is not faith without some critical judgment, but critical judgment alone will never allow me to see beyond the sometimes narrow limits of reason.

stories about the prophets. I had no reason to believe they were any different from my local leaders whom I knew to be good but ordinary humans. To me growing up, General Authorities were men in suits who spoke every six months, or at least so I was told, since I rarely went to hear them speak and did not read the *Ensign*. So early on I wasn't exactly disposed to be a strong believer in prophets. By the time I did start paying attention to what they taught, I was in the habit of approaching everything and everyone with a healthy dose of skepticism. I tested their propositions with discussion, reason, and common sense, but, initially, not with a lot of prayer.

As I described in an earlier chapter, critical judgment is a vital method for protecting myself against the dangers of groupthink and deception and for realizing the full capacity of my own conscience and powers of reason. There have been many times in church and elsewhere when I wished I had opened my mouth more. Other times I have regretted expressing myself too strongly. It's a difficult balance. The bottom line is that I can only rationally conclude that I am not always right in my rational judgments. But my critical judgment prepared me, when the time came, for a genuine witness of the divine calling of prophets and apostles. It was then that I understood that critical judgment is an even more valuable tool when it can be combined with faith and charity. Faith is not faith without some critical judgment, but critical judgment alone will never allow me to see beyond the sometimes narrow limits of reason. And as Paul counsels us, we need to learn to "[speak] the truth in love" (Ephesians 4:15).

My first witness of the calling of an apostle was in the Missionary Training Center in 1985. I was listening to Elder Dallin H. Oaks of the Quorum of the Twelve Apostles testify to a room full of missionaries there as I was preparing to leave for Venezuela as a missionary. I recall him wrapping up his talk by testifying that this was not the church of the Wasatch Front or the church of Utah or an American church, but the Church of Jesus Christ, who stood at the head. As he spoke, it felt as if a great wind blew through my hair. He bore witness of the living reality of Christ, and I could feel at that moment that all of my cultural assumptions and my shallow and young experience were not nearly enough to help me make proper judgment of what the church was or would yet be. I could see that Elder Oaks was a man, but I sensed that he was also someone who had been given a visionary understanding that was broader than his own assumptions and experiences as well. His humanity and personality were the medium, but they became less relevant than what stood behind him and spoke through him, which was the central thing. I could feel his words reaching something beyond his own ability to express. And that something seemed to me to be the ratifying presence of the Savior himself. I felt at that point I owed Elder Oaks a special kind of loyalty, although I wasn't quite sure what that meant exactly. What I was sure it didn't mean was some kind of idol worship. He was a man, a man with a story and a history not unlike many others. But I did feel that through him the Savior had been revealed to me and that I was feeling the Savior's desire to communicate to us. It certainly meant I would be reluctant to be dismissive of anything he said and that I would always want to listen for that same spirit I had felt.

A few months later I listened to Elder Neal A. Maxwell, also of the Quorum of the Twelve, for three hours teaching and testifying of Christ to a small group of us missionaries in a chapel in El Tigre, Venezuela. At this point I was less surprised by the experience because I had arrived to the mission field with greater anticipation of more revelation. I was not disappointed. I can't quite capture what I felt, but at one point I remember looking up at the ceiling, half expecting angels to come through the roof of this simple chapel. I felt so close to God and so full of love and so confident that I could become something more than I then was. I was filled with hope for my life and with gratitude for the restoration of the gospel. It wasn't an irrational frenzy of emotion for its own sake. I was sure of that. I say this because the surfeit of emotion left me hungering to live a higher law, to live more deliberately and lovingly and genuinely. I saw my life more clearly, and I could see my own potential. For this reason I knew it was of God. Of course, I felt great love for Elder Maxwell for giving me this gift. I had read many of his books and already felt that no other leader in the church had taught me quite like he had. Afterward, I was honored to shake his hand and thank him for what he had done for me. I will always remember how genuinely touched he seemed that he had made a difference for me. He too was a man, but I could feel what weighed on him, and it was Christ himself. I returned from my mission with a special regard and reverence for the experience of listening to prophets speak and testify. I can't say that I have always felt such a strong witness every time I have heard them speak, but I must admit that I haven't always hungered like I should to have Christ revealed to me. Fortunately, however, the experiences have come often enough to keep my faith strong.

One final example was listening to Elder M. Russell Ballard testify in Provo around 2001 to a group of local church leaders about the restoration of the gospel. He spoke about the presence of lost loved ones in our lives. He assured us the dead are among us, that they serve us and are concerned for our well-being. Having already had several experiences with my deceased brother's presence, I took this very much to heart. That night I had no doubt that my brother was next to me nor any doubt that another elder brother, the Savior himself, was present in the room. I say this because when Elder Ballard began to gently and lovingly call us to repentance, for a brief but clear moment I could sense that he was speaking the mind and will of Christ. This was an even more powerful witness of the special calling of an apostle than I had received previously.

As I understand the scriptures, the original apostles were special witnesses of the living Christ, the resurrected Lord. Their purpose was to counter the assumption, rational though it may have been, that Jesus was dead. They testified that the crucified man Jesus was the risen Lord and Christ, that now death and sin would no longer prevent us from returning to the presence of God. This was their commission to all the world. As I understand it, the commission of latter-day apostles is no different. I don't know what kind of witness they have received of the risen Lord, but the particular nature of that witness isn't centrally important to me. What matters is that I can feel the special power of that witness of the living Christ when they speak most directly about the Savior and when I remember to be listening for what I feel Christ wishes me to understand and do. For reasons that are known only to God and maybe in some portion to them, they are the ones the Lord has prepared, called, and chosen to give their voice to this great purpose.

Of course, church leaders have different professional backgrounds and perspectives on the issues of our day, and sometimes they speak on topics a little further afield from their witness of Christ and his gospel, as they did anciently. At those times I feel a little more removed from that core connection to the Savior that they otherwise provide, but I am glad for the opportunity to listen and learn. If I hear an occasional assertion that doesn't bring a strong ratification of the Spirit, I recognize that either I am in need of finer tuning or perhaps what I am hearing is something akin to a riff in a jazz performance that just didn't gel or a seed that was planted but didn't quite take root. It may be that the motif is picked up by another leader and might yet bear fruit. I know church leaders are careful and don't want to misrepresent the Lord. I can invariably feel and trust in that intention, but I also want to grant them the latitude to explore ideas. On a few occasions, I am aware of information about a topic that exposes to my mind the partiality of what they are saying and gives me a glimpse of their humanity. If it is true, as is often said, that they have their strong disagreements with each other on occasion, I can only imagine that they see each other's partiality often. Sometimes I have had the spiritual impression that what I am hearing is a revelation in the process of developing and the apostle or other church leader in question is still working through a question, thoughtfully and faithfully but not necessarily having achieved a fullness of understanding. Those moments move me and inspire me to want to play a proactive and sustaining role in that process of unfolding. If my confidence in the divine calling of church leaders ever wavers, I remember that although I do not share the apostle Paul's view about women speaking in church, I still believe that the power of his witness of the risen Lord is almost unparalleled. There are two things about which I am at least never in doubt: I am never in doubt about who Christ is nor in doubt about how I ought to live my life and how much more work I need to do to grow spiritually, and this knowledge is due precisely to the teachings and instructions of these special servants of the Lord.

There are certainly examples in church history of when church leaders have been wrong about one issue or another. If I were to see them as the spiritual equivalent of superheroes who have categorically superior character, superior intelligence, and superior and unassailable wisdom on all topics, then this stance would imply that the blessings and opportunities of discipleship are intended for only an elect few, which would diminish

---

My responsibility is to do what I can to keep working where I have the most direct influence to make the church as effective as it can be for others.

---

my belief in my own chances for improvement and growth. If I believe I see their weaknesses, my responsibility is to do what I can to keep working where I have the most direct influence to make the church as effective as it can be for others. This is for me more important than my judgment of the leaders or my efforts to identify discrepancies between gospel ideals and institutional culture or practice. I believe that as a member of the church, I have an obligation to make the Lord's will manifest through the Lord's anointed leaders by working for their highest vision and ideals rather than focusing on their lowest moments. To continue my jazz metaphor from earlier, great jazz ensembles know how to use mistakes and chance occurrences to create a seamlessly creative explosion of meaning and united purpose. This requires a level of comfort with occasional turbulence that is not often found in our very critical culture today. I would do myself no favors if I allowed any disagreements to overshadow my responsibility to live up to the high ideals to which those same leaders have called me and to which I have already whole-heartedly agreed.

A compelling evidence that Joseph Smith was a prophet and not a cult leader is that his first impulse was to share the burden of revelation with as many as he could.[1] He wanted everyone to see the face of God and believed that anyone could become a prophet. So how we think about prophets and seers also pertains to how we think about the lay leaders in our midst at the ward level as well as how we think of ourselves. Indeed, continuing revelation is neither necessary nor possible if we believe that one vessel is sufficiently perfect (or no vessel at all!) to trans-mit God's knowledge to his children. Why would we need more than one prophet, seer, and revelator? Why are there so many of us in this lay church, each given responsibilities as important in our sphere as those of the highest leaders? Each individual is a unique medium of the Lord's will, and this is precisely why the church depends on councils and personal revelation. Looking back over the history of a ward or stake, we cannot sum it up on the basis of just knowing the stories of the leaders. A close observation of any ward will reveal the story of hundreds of acts

---

1. Richard Bushman discusses Joseph's desire that others would receive revelation for themselves and "experience God as he did" in his book *Joseph Smith: Rough Stone Rolling* (New York: Vintage, 2007).

of compassion, hundreds of small moments of inspiration that bring healing and belonging into the lives of its members, all of which go well beyond the work of one bishop and his counselors.

It might sound counterintuitive, but I believe the best way to sustain leaders is to take some of the focus off them as examples and broaden our scope of sight so as to take in the great variety and vitality and strength of the whole body of Christ. Without that unity and loving support, the Spirit will be diminished and even the best ideas will be unlikely to have maximum benefit. In other words, if a bishop, stake president, or even an apostle has an idea but a general member of the church has information that would improve that idea, it behooves that member to speak up. But if the idea is rejected or is never received, it still behooves that member to find a way to bring out the very best results from a leader's decision. I can't imagine there is any idea a leader has that is so good it couldn't be improved upon by more carefully listening to the experiences of members of the church.

I believe we merit the revelations we receive, and if we want more we must prepare ourselves for more by squeezing every ounce of good out of current teachings and practices. Of course, in an ever larger and sometimes more bureaucratic institutional church, it is a special challenge to keep the church nimble, responsive, and focused on the essentials. But I have seen enough examples of inspired and responsive leadership and faithful and full-voiced participation by well-meaning members to keep my hope strong. This, for me, is the great call of membership. We should stay in the church because it needs the gifts and personality and life experiences of each and every one of us.

We have all noticed that different leaders get different kinds of revelations. Different bishops, it seems, get different revelations about whom to call or how to lead or whom to reach. And I suppose we could imagine that some get it right and some get it wrong, but I believe it is simultaneously true that there are many right answers for different times and according to different contexts and no answer is the last word. Even when a bishop might have made a decision without proper pursuit of the confirmation of the Lord's Spirit, as I have both witnessed and experienced myself as a bishop, the willingness of consecrated members to sustain him in his weakness will inspire them to do compensating service to minimize the damage and maybe even redeem the error. That is the case when Nephi breaks his bow and receives a negative reaction from his parents but still has the faith and love for his parents to inspire Lehi to pray to God for inspiration about what to do next (1 Nephi 16:18–24). I also believe it is possible that the Lord reveals something to a leader that is not initially fully understood by that leader but with time, input from others, and implementation becomes more clear.

There will never be just one right or perfect bishop for a ward or one right or perfect Relief Society president. And in a lay church, of course, there never is only one leader. Over the long term, sustaining means a perpetual trust, not in any one individual's skill set but in Christ, who makes of us a holy community, one body. Fortunately, leaders, indeed all members, vary in their skill sets. I have known some leaders who were especially gentle and gracious with the elderly but less skilled in reaching the youth, some who appeal to those who prefer charisma and bright personalities, and some who are quiet and reserved and more reassuring to those prone to shyness. I have known leaders whose boldness is so pronounced that they sometimes give unnecessary offense and others who are so diplomatic that they sometimes neglect to properly call out sin. In such cases these traits can be strengths or weaknesses depending on the circumstances and the faith of others. The same is true, of course, for every calling and every single one of us. Abilities, in other words, always imply disabilities as well, since other abilities are less pronounced, which means certain revelations will be more possible and others less so. When we work together and sustain each other, we allow Christ's recompenses to bless us despite our perpetual capacity for only partial success in doing God's work.

I think skeptics outside the church and even some believers within it want to imagine that the process of revelation as it is practiced by church leaders is entirely stripped of reason, deliberation, or counseling with one another. That is because, on the one hand, it makes revelation more easy to mock as an idea or, on the other, more easy to defend as a purely transcendent transmission of information from God to man. The first section of the Doctrine and Covenants makes it clear that revelation is a form of communication, not merely a transmission of information, between God and his children, and that means it involves some kind of translation from God's understanding into our own. In verse 24 we read: "Behold, I am God and have spoken it; these commandments are of me, and were given unto my servants in their weakness, after the manner of their language, that they might come to understanding." This suggests that our limited and weak human understanding is actually not an obstacle, necessarily, but an inevitable and integral part of the resulting revelation. This is not the same thing as saying that revelation is nothing but the sum total of our limited and weak understanding but merely an acknowledgement that in order for higher understanding to be made available to us, its starting place must be within the context of what we are currently able to grasp.

It also means, I suppose, that revelations are never entirely shorn of their human and earthly contexts in which they are introduced, which is why continuing revelation is needed: only through continual refinement and additional understanding and widening contexts will the fuller meaning of revelation became more visible. Revelations always come in particular times and places and contexts to specific individuals, but they are also interpreted over time and across places and contexts to others as well. It has many chances to continue to expand and grow, a process that will help us see revelations beyond their particular context and in their fuller dimensions. This is also one way of knowing when a revelation was only pertinent to a particular context and when it is much more universal. Joseph Smith's young mind interpreted the First Vision first to mean that he had been forgiven. Later, after many years of explaining it and thinking about it and with more experiences and understanding about the Restoration, it became even more apparent to him that the vision had meaning for the entire human family. Lehi's

> All of us serve more ably when we know that others are not waiting for our first misstep but are instead working quietly and steadily to assist us in reaching our potential.

dream taught the father that his sons were in trouble. The same dream, witnessed again by his son Nephi who wanted to see the same things his father did, opened up a broader vista of understanding about the plan of salvation for the human family.

In sum, we make a covenant as a community to sustain the bishop and other leaders not because they are the best individuals for the job or because we now believe they will never make a mistake but because we are bound by covenant to help the Lord do his work through all of us in our collective weaknesses. A bishop's mistakes mean that the body of the church will suffer, but if a ward suffers together in faith, those weaknesses have a chance at redemption. God knew those weaknesses as well as he knew the strengths when the bishop was called. Disunity will only make it less likely that good can be achieved. In other words, to sustain him means that we also sustain each other in our respective responsibilities so as to make him as strong as he can be. It means we expect the will of the Lord to be revealed to, and through, us. All of us serve more ably when we know that others are not waiting for our first misstep but are instead working quietly and steadily to assist us in reaching our potential, even or especially when we stand in the way of the very ideals we espouse. Each bishop and every member in every calling represents an opportunity for us to come to terms with our very human particularities that a lay church lays bare. If Christ can be seen in the countenance of this person, he can be found anywhere. And if he can't, maybe he can't be found anywhere.

In the rare event that a bishop or any other church leader is guilty of a serious offense and poses any real danger to members, I believe that members are not only no longer under the obligation to sustain but, for the sake of the health of that same body of Christ, actively responsible for speaking up, to the degree that they are aware of the offense, so as to remove this individual from a position of trust. Alma counsels, "Trust no one to be your teacher nor your minister, except he be a man of God, walking in his ways and keeping his commandments" (Mosiah 23:14). This is not an invitation to criticize a leader's every misstep, but it is a reminder that the very purpose of soliciting a sustaining vote is to provide the chance for the expression of serious concerns. Sustaining a church leader does not mean looking away, tolerating, or justifying abuse of power and trust.

If the recent flood of excitement about the calling of our first Latin American and first Asian American apostles is any indication, members of the church are ready to welcome more diversity among church leaders. I think it is natural and good to be aware of the ways that we are limited by gender, nationality, age, class, race, and so on. I am not reassured by suggestions that such differences don't matter. We should be aware of the limitations of homogeneity in the church and do the work necessary to compensate for any weaknesses that might ensue. In 3 Nephi 15, we read that Christ did not tell his apostles about the other sheep because of their "stiffneckedness and unbelief" (v. 18). Surely their refusal to imagine other possibilities was a function of their cultural and geographical homogeneity. Besides, if such differences didn't matter, why would we need diversity at all? Why would God have even bothered to create so much? Why would he insist that a man and a woman sealed together is the highest covenant we can make? Any group, large or small, of people who share the same gender or race or class or nationality will only run higher risks of failing to consider alternatives to their own instincts. Diversity is the key to the growth of understanding and the fuller restoration of truth. I am not saying it is inevitable or necessary that women get the priesthood or that we someday must have an African apostle, for example, although I see no reason to believe that either scenario is undesirable or impossible. I have no idea what the Lord intends, nor do I want to pretend that I do. I am thrilled to sustain what the Lord has deemed to be the structure of his church today. I simply see no reason to get overly defensive when these valuable and valid questions are raised. I only hope they are not raised simply to create doubt in the church and its current leaders.

Besides, to prize diversity isn't to say that the work of the Lord cannot be done in the context of homogeneity. If that were the case, it would have never happened in any context whatsoever. Christ's original disciples could hardly be described as diverse. Despite their weakness, Christ called them nevertheless and they did his work, which tells me that we shouldn't let the ambition for greater diversity and inclusion override our primary obligation to sustain whom the Lord calls. In my experience in the humanities, I believe that diversity matters because it helps us confront the individual and particular stories of each person. It helps us see our humanity. So it is contradictory to desire more diversity in church leadership but then refuse to see and sustain the particular humanity of the individual church leaders we currently have precisely because of their backgrounds and circumstances. Not to mention the fact that such attitudes can override or ignore the divine authority by which these leaders have been called, the very authority that supposedly matters enough to some critics to argue for its more widely distributed use. My point is that we can and should ask questions, but if we act as if divine authority can be redistributed without divine sanction, we contradict the meaning of such authority. Besides, the scandal of particularity is the most important message of Christianity. That God would become flesh, born in particular circumstances in an ordinary town or ordinary occupation, is utterly scandalous. So we might say that it is a scandal to believe that men can hold the priesthood and God's work can still move forward, just as it is to believe that the Savior could be a carpenter's son.

Speaking of scandal, twice now I have been called to serve as an ecclesiastical leader. And on both occasions my name was announced and the congregation had a matter of seconds to decide to vote in support of me but did so unanimously. Kind notes and expressions of faith followed, helping to shore up my own state of astonishment that the Lord would have chosen me. I felt the most profound gratitude for God's trust but just as importantly for the trust of the members who, apparently without much hesitation as far as I could tell, accepted the will of the Lord. And in both cases, I can say that I was not 100 percent confident in my ability to lead. But I was 100 percent certain that I was *not* asked to lead. I was asked to be a conduit *to allow the*

Lord to lead. I am also 100 percent certain that I have not had the confidence 100 percent of the time that I am doing the Lord's will. But because his is the voice I have at least sought to hear in my weakness, I have felt strengthened by the faith of others that I can succeed. That is perhaps the single most important difference with our worldly definitions of leadership. I certainly am capable of getting in the way. I would do my parishioners no favors to pretend otherwise, but I also appreciate the collective faith that we might all come to a higher understanding through the order of the church that the Lord has established.

When such a calling happens to you—you whose appreciation for your own weaknesses and limitations is especially keen—you feel profound gratitude for the faith of others who trust that your particulars (in my case a white middle-class male with a particular life journey I shared in an earlier essay) will not stand in the way of the Lord's will. Their faith might go so far as to believe that your set of life experiences might even be needed in the particular circumstances your ward or stake finds itself in. In my experience such faith grants an added source of power to a leader that helps revelations to come much more easily. I can say this much: those hands raised in support signify not a vote in favor of a person but an expression of faith that together we can hope for the Lord's guidance in our lives as we work together in doing the Lord's work. If asked if my call as an ecclesiastical leader was rational, I would laugh. But I must testify that I know that the Lord called me. I won't share all the reasons why I know this. They are too personal, but I was initially as surprised as anyone. That might sound like false humility, but it is true. So if anyone had a right to complain, it was me. But the point is, it will always be a particular person in a particular calling that will require our sustaining vote, and such votes are expressions of confidence not so much in the person but in the possibility of revelation. When revelation comes and the faithful receive it, it doesn't matter who the conduit is or what that person's particulars might be. What matters, what is all-important, is the living God whose love our collective faith makes available to us.

Let me conclude with a thought about trust and waiting from the story of Adam and Eve. I have always found it curious that when they were in the garden, they initially got more information from Satan than they did from God. Satan was not interested in withholding information, whereas the Lord

---

Christianity teaches the paradox that there is wisdom in accepting our foolishness, strength in accepting our weaknesses and limitations, power in accepting our powerlessness.

---

seemed intent on creating the conditions for a kind of probation. What Satan wanted was their loyalty, even if it meant he had to reveal God's secrets. "Ye shall not surely die," he exclaimed, "ye shall be as gods, knowing good and evil" (Moses 4:10–11). On its face this is a perfectly rational and truthful answer to Eve's somewhat incomplete understanding of what would happen if she ate the fruit. All the Lord had said at that point was that they would die. That wasn't untrue, but it is fair to ask, Why hadn't the Lord explained his plan a little more clearly? Why had he not explained that eating the fruit of the tree of knowledge would open an entire world of learning and experience for them? Would it have hurt his purposes to explain to them that understanding would come soon enough but only in the process of practicing their obedience to the Lord?

Apparently, it would have. God was intent on teaching the universal truth that in this mortal experiment we must choose to act and choose our paths in life with, at best, incomplete information. What he wanted was to provide assurances that obedience and faithfulness to his revealed word would provide a pathway through the times of darkness and confusion that such conditions give us. He never promised we would have full understanding here and now. What he promised was that faithfulness would bring deeper understanding and trust, goodness and blessings of joy in circumstances that would otherwise make us miserable, and that this would prepare us for eternal progress toward his understanding of all things. When asked why he performs sacrifices, Adam answers, "I know not, save the Lord commanded me" (Moses 5:6). Adam was obedient, but perhaps we could understand his obedience more importantly as an act of faithfulness, as a kind of conscious loyalty. He would come to understand the purpose of his sacrifice in the practice of it, as an emulation of the sacrifice of the Son of God, but only after careful performance of an act that was required as a sign of his loyalty to the Lord. Mere verbal reassurances of such loyalty would never suffice. It had to be an action and a sacrificial one at that.

In contrast to this slow accretion of divinely revealed truth, the knowledge that Satan offers comes free of charge. There is nothing required—no act, no submission, no wager of faith, and consequently no personal growth. This means that if we are impatient with the incomplete information revealed to us and we refuse to trust or act in faith, then we can become vulnerable to the temptations of free and easy information, knowledge that we imagine can fill the gap of our understandings and allow us to make decisions without wagers of faith. We sometimes prefer a God of clear instruction who does not ask us to struggle with meaning but who will provide knowledge cost-free. We will pretend, in other words, as so many of us do, that we can act in the world with sufficient and complete knowledge and that we should therefore never be asked or expected to act otherwise. What I mean to suggest is the danger of assuming we have to have or already have sufficient understanding before we can act rightly, meaningfully, and faithfully in the world. Critics of religion, and sometimes its most zealous defenders, pretend as if there is a world in which we can act without the risk of foolishness. Christianity teaches the paradox that there is wisdom in accepting our foolishness, strength in accepting our weaknesses and limitations, power in accepting our powerlessness. And what it requires above all is not understanding or right thinking but love. And what it gives in response to our patient faithfulness is transformation of ourselves and the world. As Isaiah promises so beautifully, "They that wait upon the Lord shall renew their strength; they shall mount up with wings as eagles" (Isaiah 40:31).

I fully understand that a belief in living prophets makes little or no sense to my academic peers and to many people in the world. But I believe I have an obligation of loyalty to them as special messengers from the Lord and this loyalty manifests itself by patient waiting on the Lord, a willingness to forgo the sniffing out of error in fallible men and instead a desire to cultivate an understanding of what portion, large or small, of truth I can glean from their words. I insist that I do not believe it is disloyal to ask questions or to even express open disagreement. Indeed, precisely because obedience does not require but instead rewards with understanding, I am wary of easy or superficially logical explanations that try to make facile sense of things that do not deserve superficiality but instead require time and patience and faithful waiting. I could obey for lots of wrong reasons of my own making, and this, I doubt, is a virtue. For that matter, it may not be a virtue, either, to obey without a desire for understanding, without anticipation of some new understanding to come. I am generally suspicious of claims in my own heart that I think I know what a servant of the Lord should say or what the church should do. I have no interest in seeking to trap a church leader in a logical contradiction. I cannot understand any conception of truth that does not allow for its multifaceted and many-layered qualities nor require many different voices and personalities to give it fuller expression. I think it is possible, maybe even inevitable, that an assertion together with its counterassertion can capture aspects of a larger truth that stands above them both. That is one reason why I am also suspicious of explanations that are generated just to justify polemical positions and reduce our own anxieties about what we do not yet understand. I am eager to see the day when church members have finally learned how to ask probing questions and even identify the terms of their disagreement in a true spirit of unity and love and commitment, when loyalty will be understood not just as a protection of what we have received but as a collaborative search for greater light and understanding.

I suspect that it matters far more how much love we retain in our hearts for God and for our fellow men and women than what we think or how we reason our way through social and political issues. Ideas matter, but love matters more, and love is an action that we render out of trust in what is good about others and about life and about God himself. Love might be the answer, as the saying goes, but it isn't an answer per se. It is a feeling of trust, a way of waiting, faithfully, with loyalty, a patient suffering that does not despair at having insufficient answers but instead trusts that with or without them we can with loyalty know in whom we trust. Satan is perfectly willing to give us the truth if we are impatient enough to accept it without love, without sacrifice, just to allow us the privilege of feeling that we are right. He will gladly trade such truths for hatred in our hearts; he will happily talk truth all night long if he can get us to stop loving others with forbearance and to start judging them with harshness. What a waste it would be if he can get us to stop waiting faithfully on the Lord for understanding we do not yet possess and for powers of love we cannot naturally summon.

Politics, Religion, and the Pursuit of Community

I admire those who speak up and speak out. I admire those who work to stay informed about political and institutional matters because they understand that institutions need vigilance. I see nothing wrong with a healthy demonstration of political opposition or discontent with the status quo. In fact, a healthy democracy is inconceivable without a widespread and passionate concern for justice among people. Apathy, indifference, and ignorance seem to provide the greatest assurance that abuses of power will emerge and continue unchecked. I was recently elected to the city council of my hometown, and I can attest to the fact that vigilant public comment doesn't just prevent abuses of power, it enhances the chances for wise and good legislation.

Of course, the problem is that, as one friend of mine recently observed of his Latter-day Saint ward, we can be a united and civil community one moment and suddenly a policy issue emerges front and center and that unity can shatter into a thousand pieces. Only an aggressive and undemocratic suppression of voices could create the illusion that consensus or unity is easy. Free and open societies render differing or even oppositional views of justice, thus making it difficult to achieve what one believes to be right and just. While democracy depends on advocacy, advocacy is precarious because of how easily it can lead to

> To have empathetic understanding
> of the roots of anger, of course, doesn't
> mean that in all cases we have to agree
> with or justify such anger; it only means
> that we allow for the possibility
> of being instructed by it.

a kind of deafness to alternative experiences or ideas. Thus it is tempting, especially for those with low tolerance for other points of view or conflict, to become impatient with or exhausted by democracy. And this can lead to a withdrawal from the civic sphere or to a willingness to use intimidation, bullying, and incivility to get what one wants. It can even lead to compromise on fundamental protections for a free press and free expression. But if apathy is unacceptable, so too is a refusal to empathize with or understand the roots of someone else's anger. The fact that someone is red hot and uncivil about an injustice is not sufficient reason to conclude that the injustice is not real. What we need, then, is a balance of conviction and forbearance, or what the Chilean author Antonio Skármeta once called a "burning patience."[1]

---

1.   Antonio Skármeta, *Burning Patience* (New York: Pantheon, 1987).

I think what often worries people about empathy is that it seems like a slippery slope. Once we start empathizing with our enemy, we start identifying ourselves with that person, and before we know it, we are convinced that person is right. And if our enemy has been hateful or abusive toward us, our empathy can risk becoming a form of internalized self-hatred. Indeed, love of one's enemy should not supersede love of oneself. But love of oneself is not complete without at least being able to see and understand one's enemy as a fellow human and being able to understand the roots of the behavior that causes us so much difficulty. To have empathetic understanding of the roots of anger, of course, doesn't mean that in all cases we have to agree with or justify such anger; it only means that we allow for the possibility of being instructed by it. I don't know why we wouldn't be better off as a nation if we could simultaneously understand, for example, the roots of anger that propelled Donald Trump to the presidency and the roots of anger that propelled millions of women into the streets in the aftermath.

My argument isn't with anger per se. Rather it is with the assumption that anger and resistance to institutions or perceived enemies are always either the best or only viable path to social change. My argument is with the tendency to see government, universities, religions, other public institutions, and even other people as merely there to serve us, almost like airlines, where we hope for nothing more than to be able to sit back, relax, and enjoy the flight. From the outside, or perhaps from an increasingly large and complex web of bureaucracy on the inside, we speak glibly and derisively of those who run large organizations. Institutional abuses are real, so there are important reasons for distrust, but if the examples of our greatest fighters for change teach us anything, distrust should be a great motivator for more-engaged stewardship and less-dismissive detachment. My argument is with distrust or apathy that is born of our self-obsessed, entertainment- and pleasure-driven culture or ignorance and indifference about the good that institutions are striving to do. When fewer people are voting and fewer still seem even remotely informed about or engaged in public affairs, it is no wonder that abuses go unchecked. We forget that governments, like most any institution (including The Church of Jesus Christ of Latter-day Saints), consist of people and thrive when they are nurtured by a deep impulse within us to give, rather than merely receive, service. If we don't work at their care and proper functioning, we will only make matters worse.

So while I honor our tradition of demonstrations and protests, I worry about a citizenry that, because it is too reactive and thinks of such actions only when faced with injustice, has neglected the many proactive, creative, and lifelong commitments and actions that have proved effective in strengthening institutions, democracy, and the conditions for sustainable change. I am thinking of such commitments as lifelong reading and education from various sources about politics and history; informed and regular voting; civic engagement at local, state, or national levels; vital and diverse nonprofit work; running for office; promoting thoughtful culture and arts; and many other related efforts that help build a good society. In Mosiah we read that "it is not common that the voice of the people desireth anything contrary to that which is right; but it is common for the lesser part of the people to desire that which is not right" (Mosiah 29:26). As social science research also indicates, the best decisions are made when there is greater participation from more diverse and more informed voices. Wider participation and listening also mean we are less likely to become unnecessarily polarized in our views of a problem and more willing to identify and work for practical solutions. Factionalism, in other words, only diminishes our chances to get things right.

Instead, what we see now are absurd depths of partisan bickering and radical suspicion toward other people's "facts" and disturbing trends toward apathy and disengagement. These two phenomena mutually reinforce each other. Opposition and difference of opinion are natural and normal. But what has prevented us from thoughtfully engaging our differences is the fact that we have sold our political and deliberative souls to ideologies that do our thinking for us. We are peddled positions and postures that are offered as eternal pillars of Truth, even though any quick glance at history demonstrates how fickle and arbitrary party lines really are.

Since differences these days are seen as things to announce and lines to be drawn rather than opportunities for forming relationships and solving problems, it is no wonder that many prefer the ease and comfort of like-minded echo chambers. Real engagement with our differences requires a kind of work that partisan ideology shields us from: the hard work of swimming upstream to educate oneself and overcome inherited biases and misunderstandings; to read one's news and not just watch or listen to pundits; and to work out differences with others in a spirit of civility. The problem is that the longer we forestall such work, the more likely it will be that when we are forced to try to confront our differences, such experiences will only result in more ugliness and reinforce our preference to retreat to our tribalistic comfort zones.

In short, without a more engaged citizenry, we have allowed political parties, or "factions" as our founding fathers knew them, to dictate what we should care about, and this in turn has led to more extremism and less compromise. Why, for example, do so many conservatives turn their backs on their own proud tradition and have such contempt for conservation? Why, on the other hand, do so many progressives ignore the religious roots of their very own convictions and see religion with such disdain? One can scarcely think of a political issue today that has not become polarized and distorted, as if in a funny mirror, by partisan fighting. Even though study after study shows how profoundly irrational political beliefs often are, how deeply embedded they are in our psyche and instincts, we nevertheless grant them an authority that no man or woman of conscience or of religious conviction ever ought to countenance. Time after time, a complex issue that can be solved only by careful listening, negotiation, and compromise is reduced to simple formulas that appeal to predetermined and oppositional partisan solutions. And then we find ourselves and others believing and behaving in ways that resemble more and more the worst stereotype the other side has and less and less the norms of a reflective Christian life.

In order to reengage, we need to find a way to react to the incivility we see without detachment, apathy, or further incivility. It would be good, I think, to remember what it is that we are pursuing as a nation and as a church as well. In both cases our objective is not personal or tribal gain but the elusive and all-important goal of community. Community is not possible without the foundational practice of forbearance and charity grounded in a profound and reverent appreciation for every human being as "a son or daughter of heavenly parents with a divine nature and destiny."[2]

We also need to refuse to perpetuate the flippancy and superficiality of the political rhetoric—usually devoid of any context or substance that would allow for any kind of serious analysis—that gets tossed back and forth with such ease on talk radio, cable news, and the Internet and that also gets passed along through

---

2. "The Family: A Proclamation to the World," The Church of Jesus Christ of Latter-day Saints, Salt Lake City, Utah, September 23, 1995.

email, Facebook posts, tweets, and offhanded comments. In a BYU Forum titled "The Hard Work of Understanding the Constitution," Thomas Griffith recently warned students:

> Harold McMillan—prime minister of Great Britain and chancellor of Oxford University from 1960 to 1986—described the primary purpose of a university education to the graduating class at Oxford: "Nothing you learn here at Oxford will be of the slightest possible use to you later, save only this: if you work hard and intelligently, you should be able to detect when a man is talking rot. And that is the main, if not the sole, purpose of education." If your education at BYU hasn't helped you see that such partisan talk is "rot," then you have failed in your studies. And I'm not kidding.[3]

Precisely because of their tendency to perpetuate and solidify error, the "traditions of the fathers" should be subject to rigorous scrutiny and, if necessary, bold rejection.

I have found that it is especially hard for students to separate the "rot" from true wisdom when many of their chosen role models are themselves spinners of so much frantic bloviating. I sorrow when I see students who seem afraid to come into contact

---

3. Thomas B. Griffith, "The Hard Work of Understanding the Constitution," Brigham Young University forum address, Provo, Utah, September 18, 2012.

with new ideas for no other reason than it would disappoint someone they care about. President Thomas S. Monson has wisely said that we should never let a problem that needs solving be more important than a person who needs love.[4] It is probably also true that we should never allow a relationship with someone we love dictate how and what we think. Christ made that very apparent; in one of his hardest teachings, he expects us to have the courage to depart from family if family relationships stand in the way of truth. If we are to be true Christians, we must, to use the words of Mormon, "lay hold upon every good thing" (Moroni 7:19); we must be as serious about embracing good ideas as identifying bad ones regardless of the wishes of others. I can think of a no small number of examples of false folk beliefs that have emerged in Latter-day Saint culture over time and were based more on prejudice than on doctrine and perpetuated more by loyalty to family and individual role models than by faith or reason. As the story of the Book of Mormon shows, such teachings become traditions when they become intergenerational, and they can take a great deal of time, expense, and struggle to eradicate. Precisely because of their tendency to perpetuate and solidify error, the "traditions of the fathers" should be subject to rigorous scrutiny and, if necessary, bold rejection (see Helaman 15:4; Doctrine and Covenants 93:39).

Of course, it is much easier to detect "rot" and partisan blindness when it is manifested by our political opponents or when it attempts to attack our community and our interests. And therein lies the rub. What is the secret to an education that can empower us to be able to discern rot not only across the aisle but also in our own like-minded circles or, even more importantly, *in our own thinking*? One particularly dangerous thing about

---

4. Thomas S. Monson, "Finding Joy in the Journey," *Ensign*, November 2008, 86.

partisan thinking is its seduction that there is categorical safety in thinking in a certain kind of way about complex social and political problems. As a humanist and as a Christian, I find such logic offensive to common sense. For liberals and conservatives both, there is the very real danger of political ideology becoming more centrally important to one's identity, values, and relationships than one's commitments to basic Christian doctrine.

And what is more fundamental than the Sermon on the Mount? Jesus tells us that our strength does not come from what we know, what we are, or what we possess but in recognizing what we lack. Moreover, he tells us to love our enemies, to bless those who persecute us. Does this mean we should stand aside in the face of evil and let ourselves or others be abused? Should we become apathetic about justice? Jesus certainly never did. But along with a commitment to justice, our Christian duty, it seems to me, should include a careful cultivation of an awareness of our weakness and of what we lack, even if this runs counter to seemingly every self-affirming and evil-denouncing impulse in a partisan society such as ours. Every great musician plays wrong notes. Every great athlete fumbles and stumbles. Every hitter strikes out. And every great moral thinker is capable of being terribly wrong. Griffith cites Oliver Cromwell on this point: "I beseech ye in the bowels of Christ; think ye might be mistaken."[5] The dangerous seduction of getting a little information and being partly right—but believing we have all the information or are all the way right—is what Isaiah describes as wisdom in our own eyes (see Isaiah 5:21). We end up believing that just because we have high ideals, we are incapable of wrong judgment.

The function of Christian belief is not merely to shore up confidence about moral principles and transcendent truths but

---

5. Quoted in Griffith, "Hard Work of Understanding the Constitution." The quotation comes from a letter of Oliver Cromwell to the General Assembly of the Kirk of Scotland, August 3, 1650.

also to accept the challenge that in our earnest devotion to and defense of them we might, at times, *betray them*. We must be on guard, as we are warned in the opening section of the Doctrine and Covenants, to avoid "walk[ing] in [our] own way, and after the image of [our] own god" (1:16). The possibility of such betrayal shouldn't surprise us. This is a story as old as the gospel itself. God is not to be doubted, but to be Christian, to have Christian faith, requires a willingness to engage in *self*-doubt. What is even more important than obedience to and knowledge of the law, in other words, is a devotion to repentance, and this is because it is our natural limitation to be imperfect in our obedience and in our understandings of the truth. It is also natural to want to shape our minds and wills after an idea of God that conforms to our natural instincts.

Incivility is often grounded in a worldview that is Manichaean and in a tendency to objectify and dehumanize opponents. It is us against them. Good versus evil. The right versus the wrong. Forgive the irony, but there are two problems with such worldviews. We might mistakenly assume we are in the right. And we might mistakenly assume we aren't. As Isaiah so eloquently says, "Woe unto them that call evil good, and good evil; that put darkness for light, and light for darkness; that put bitter for sweet, and sweet for bitter! Woe unto them that are wise in their own eyes, and prudent in their own sight!" (Isaiah 5:20–21). It is never enough, in other words, just to identify error or falsehood. It is not enough to fight or stand up for what is right. We must be as assiduously devoted to overturning the soils of tradition to identify and embrace the good. This is a two-pronged duty; as the Lord commands, "Forsake all evil *and* cleave unto all good" (Doctrine and Covenants 98:11; emphasis added). Even though the gospel asks us to sift the good from the evil, we have to be about the work of both forsaking evil and cleaving unto good or we will do neither. In other words, if we think that evil and good are already patently obvious, complete with warning labels and other easily identifiable markers, and that the judgment to know one from the other doesn't require the risk of experimentation or experience, we deny the entire purpose of the Fall. If we always assume the world can be easily divided, we might end up seeing differences as categorically threatening the very fabric and foundation of our community. Differences, however, and even our enemies are often what enable us to become a stronger and healthier community when we see them as opportunities to learn and overcome ourselves. Maintaining a healthy democracy and building Zion both require finding a way to make diversity into a strength, not a weakness.

The Sermon on the Mount raises the question: what would it take to perceive our political opponents not as enemies but as friends? Would this mean that we must accept abuse or injustice? I do not believe love of our enemies implies passivity or internalization of hatefulness aimed at us. Seeing and understanding the roots of opposition from others doesn't mean agreement, nor does it mean we have to drop our own cause. It *might* mean these things, but only to the degree that we warrant correction. But it might mean that we continue with even more confidence that we are fighting for the right cause, and such increase in confidence might be one of the benefits of our effort to reach understanding. Whatever the outcome of striving to love our enemies, we will have been able to check our tendencies toward judgment blinded by vitriol and dehumanization. This will have no small influence on the quality of our own judgments.

I have lived in Berkeley, California, one of the most liberal places in the nation, and I currently live in Provo, Utah, one of the most conservative. I think it is safe to say that I have witnessed the damages of partisan extremism on both sides. On the left, I have seen the excesses of liberal thought that cannot acknowledge the legitimacy of fundamental conservative principles such as freedom or fiscal responsibility. I have also seen how liberal secularism often rejects wholesale the legitimacy of religious, particularly Christian, experience or thought. On the right, I have seen similar excesses of conservative thinking that refuses to consider justice or fairness and is blind to compassion. In its more sectarian forms, such conservativism ends up seeing each and every difference as an insidious effort to overturn all that is good and right in the world. In both cases, there is a vulnerability to conspiratorial paranoia. I don't mean to suggest there

---

Why should we ever assume any political platform is safe or undeserving of careful scrutiny? What do we put at risk when we abdicate the responsibility to be critical and vigilant about the allures of ideology?

---

is no truth found on the outer edges of the political spectrum. I only mean to underscore the ways in which political and religious homogeneity can stimulate chauvinism and intolerance and protect us from ever having to know or interact with anyone who is different.

Why should we ever assume any political platform is safe or undeserving of careful scrutiny? What do we put at risk when we abdicate the responsibility to be critical and vigilant about the allures of ideology? For one thing, we end up risking support for policies or politicians, in the name of our highest ideals, that consistently violate those ideals. It's tempting to imagine that if

I am living right as a member of the church, my political beliefs must also be sanctioned by God. Why, then, do good people disagree? Why, for that matter, do believers sometimes lack wisdom and nonbelievers sometimes prove capable of good works? Elder D. Todd Christofferson, in a worldwide training for church leaders, taught the following:

> There doesn't have to be an agreement on all points of doctrine for us to collaborate with and work with others. My own experience is that I'm a better person through that kind of association. I've had many opportunities in the different places that I've lived around the country and outside the U.S. *to work with other groups, people of other faiths and, in some cases, no faith, I suppose, but people of real goodwill.* And as I said, I feel like I'm a better man for it. And the Church organization really lends itself to group service. Our quorums and wards and all the organizations really do *facilitate and prepare us to lead out and, in some cases, to join others.*[6]

We are stronger, in other words, when we are not going it alone. To use partisan or religious litmus tests on candidates makes a mockery of both the hard work that personal revelation entails and the hard work that democracy requires. It also tends to produce superficial and sometimes dangerous assumptions about God's hidden purposes.

I remember a conservative Mormon friend telling me all the way back in 1984 that she was going to vote for Ronald Reagan for no more reason than because she knew that he prayed. I had no reason to doubt he did. But Walter Mondale was the son of a minister, and Reagan was an actor and our first divorced president, so I could imagine someone supporting Mondale

---

6. D. Todd Christofferson, "The Gospel Answers Life's Problems and Challenges," Worldwide Leadership Training, interview by L. Tom Perry, January 2012; emphasis added.

with exactly the same logic, which told me that she was using an arbitrary and potentially mischievous litmus test. To the best of my understanding, despite different opinions people might have about their policies, one of the most believing and practicing Christian presidents in recent history appears to be Barack Obama and one of the least appears to be Donald Trump. If it seems that judgment is so much more difficult than the use of simplistic reasoning, it's because it *is* so much more difficult. This is to say that maybe some humility, some listening to one another, and a little less certainty are in order.

However, we are uncomfortable with the burden of being responsible for building true community. It is hard work to be a citizen. We need to be confident in the uniqueness of our own story and perspective and to speak from a place of authenticity. We can't truly know ourselves, however, if we don't know those who are different from us. Courage to speak up must also be accompanied by a commitment to reading and listening a lot. And I don't mean reading a lot from the same source, over and over again, just because it confirms our previously held opinions or because it provides good zingers and sound bites. I certainly don't mean reading according to the echoing algorithms of Facebook. I mean that we should read, in John Milton's term, "promiscuously,"[7] searching beyond the comfort of our own familiar thinking and our nearest and most intimate circle of like-minded people. We cannot afford to be fearful of contrary ideas, as if the very existence of contradiction threatens the truths we hold so dear. If truth is truth, it has nothing whatsoever to fear; it is only rendered less meaningful and less true if we feel it is our duty to shield it or protect it from any contact with other ideas. Faith in the truth means having the courage to

---

7. John Milton, *Areopagitica*, in *The Norton Anthology of English Literature*, ed. Stephen Greenblatt et al. (New York: W. W. Norton, 2006), 713.

talk to and be friends with people who have views different from our own. It means not just tepid tolerance of difference but a profound understanding that truth shines more powerfully and the best policies emerge through broad exposure to and experimentation with a plurality of ideas.

Given our early history as a persecuted religious minority and our more recent history in US politics, Latter-day Saints ought to be especially vigilant about mischievous religious and partisan litmus tests. I remember how Mike Huckabee handled Romney's faith in Romney's first campaign. He was cagey, even brilliant, in the way he played on Evangelical fears about Latter-day Saints to subtly suggest that Romney's religious persuasion disqualified him for the job. Was "Mormonism" a religion or a cult? he was asked. "I think it's a religion. [He *thinks* it's a religion?!] I don't really know that much about it. Don't Mormons believe Jesus and the devil are brothers?"[8] In Romney's second run, faced with the task of supporting a Latter-day Saint candidate for office, Huckabee reversed his position for the sake of party loyalty and said to the nation at the Republican National Convention: "Let me clear the air about whether guys like me would only support an evangelical," he said. "Of the four people on the two tickets, the only self-professed evangelical is Barack Obama, and he supports changing the definition of marriage, believes that human life is disposable and expendable at any time in the womb or even beyond the womb, and tells people of faith that they must bow their knees to the god of government and violate their faith and conscience in order to comply with what he calls healthcare." Cartoon characterizations of Obama's positions aside, he implies that his ecumenical spirit is somehow an exception, not a rule, to democracy in a plural society. "I care

---

8. Quoted in Joanne Kenen, "Huckabee Questions Tenet of Romney's Mormon Faith," *Reuters*, December 12, 2007, https://www.reuters.com/article/us-usa-politics-huckabee-religion-lif-idUSN1210277520071213.

far less," he says as if announcing a new principle of fairness, "as to where Mitt Romney takes his family to church than I do about where he takes this country."[9]

I believe that religion is relevant to politics, but it seems to be so in a paradoxical way. Christ as well as the apostle James, to name just two examples, made it all too clear that it is one thing to believe and another altogether to act on that belief. James suggests that when belief functions to blind us from truly seeing ourselves honestly and self-critically, we are vulnerable to self-deception. James writes: "But be ye doers of the word, and not hearers only, deceiving your own selves. For if any be a hearer of the word, and not a doer, he is like unto a man beholding his natural face in a glass: for he beholdeth himself, and goeth his way, and straightway forgetteth what manner of man he was" (James 1:22–24). It is dangerous to hitch our wagon of belief to the star of identity. By that I mean the purpose of belief is not to be an affirmation or marker of identity of who we think we already are or an indication that we are already who we want to become; rather, belief challenges the very idea of a fixed identity. We are not born good or bad, nor for that matter inherently talented, intelligent, religious or inherently not. We are born free, free to choose and to become far better than we are. Belief is an instrument of growth and change, not a label of fixity. It points to an aspiration, not a conclusion, that we announce to others when we declare belief. In its essence, the declaration of Christian faith suggests a man or woman who has accepted their brokenness and placed their hope for change in Christ. Christianity in a politician is no longer a mark of such confessed brokenness. Rather, it functions more today like the kinds of signs Christ criticized us for sometimes seeking: it is

---

9. Mike Huckabee, speech at the Republican National Convention, August 29, 2012.

an arbitrary label that nevertheless is supposed to offer a reliable sign of being in the right so that we don't have to assume any of the inherent risks of belief.

Factionalism and religious litmus tests were never intended to drive the political process. But here we are in the twenty-first century in a remarkably diverse nation and we are as factionally polarized and anxious and fearful about religion as ever. I would suggest this is because Americans have not yet cultivated

The tragedy of our American political scene is that Christian virtues have been divided against themselves in the two major parties, as if being both passionate about tolerance *and* uncompromising in the pursuit of truth were inconsistent with what it means to be a Christian.

a definition of community that is generous enough to the reality of our history. None of this is to say that religious belief is irrelevant to politics, but I do mean to suggest that its relevance is not only in terms of what kinds of policies it might motivate but more importantly in terms of what kind of community it can imagine and aspire to build. I believe in the old virtues of recognizing weakness, loving enemies, exercising forbearance, showing forth compassion and patience, and seeking out the good in all people, virtues that were supposed to be the very core of Christian values. Christian beliefs allow for impassioned advocacy or even protest, but precisely because Christianity defends the defenseless, protects the vulnerable, and is vigilant about the stranger, it is sad and surprising that it hasn't inspired more activism on behalf of the disadvantaged. It is also sad and surprising that Christianity isn't that force, absent in political parties, that can balance the ever-important pursuit of justice with the equally important commitment to mercy, forgiveness, and compassion. Indeed, the tragedy of our American political scene is that Christian virtues have been divided against themselves in the two major parties, as if being both passionate about tolerance *and* uncompromising in the pursuit of truth were inconsistent with what it means to be a Christian. Even the very definition of justice is so divided that it creates the illusion that one cannot care simultaneously for black lives and police officers, the unborn and the rights of women, the strength of family and marriage and the plight of LGBT individuals, the well-being of those born into intergenerational poverty, and the degradation of the Creation.

All this suggests that one of the most Christian acts we Christians, especially those of us who enjoy the highest benefits of modern living and well-being, can perform is to willingly lay down our swords of righteous indignation and obsessions with weeding out errors of belief from our culture and pick up the ploughshares required to build good and decent and fair communities. I believe in the right and responsibility to announce my Christianity. I think John Lennon's utopia of a world without religion is a farce. But sometimes being Christian paradoxically involves an ability to work indistinguishably in solidarity with any person of goodwill. This goes beyond saying to oneself begrudgingly, "I don't like these people, I don't agree with these people, and I hope someday they will just go away, but I will work with them for the time being." Being Christian means having to acknowledge the gap between our wisdom and God's, between our understanding of how God works in our lives or in national and international affairs and who God actually is or what he actually does. Believing in God sometimes means having to acknowledge the possibility that we are often wrong about him because we are too biased by nationalism, or even by just our background and upbringing, and not yet fully versed in the workings of God across vast swaths of peoples and cultures. Believing in God means having to acknowledge that he gets his work done through processes, exchanges, and many, many people of all stripes and cultures and beliefs, far beyond our reckoning.

I don't pretend to speak for God or know much about what he wants for this country or for international affairs, but I am pretty sure he does not have a political party. I am also persuaded that he is more aware than parties and powers in the world of the plight of the millions of his children in extreme poverty, the flagging health of his creation, the ongoing senseless violence among nations, the abuse and degradation of women and human sexuality, and the arrogance and pride of the wealthy. I say this because I have spent my time reading my Old Testament and the Book of Mormon. But I am nevertheless never certain that my political beliefs line up with his, if indeed he has any. I don't mean to suggest that I think he doesn't want us to have political passions. Because political convictions have the potential to make the world a better place, then I have to believe they are relevant to his concerns. But I am also pretty sure that it is easy to be right about lots of particular political causes without being a particularly good person and that he seems to care more about the latter than the former.

If we can begin to acknowledge that God is as intimately involved in our lives, our community, and our nation as he is in the lives of the most different human communities here and elsewhere, then we can face the ultimate paradox of belief. Belief roots us in an understanding of God and our place in the world, but it does not serve its deepest purpose if such rooting takes place in willful ignorance or disdain for populations with stories radically different from our own. They too are God's creations, his equally treasured children. "Know ye not that there are more nations than one?" Nephi asks (2 Nephi 29:7). It is incumbent on believers to be respectful and curious about the hidden purposes of such diversity.

Will American Christianity merely tepidly tolerate the nation's or the world's diversity? Have we grown tired of being an immigrant nation and now prefer a refueled and false nativism? Can we learn more about our Creator by taking advantage of our cultural and political diversity and commit to listen to and learn the stories of those most different from us? Can we see their human dignity and appreciate their own pursuit of what is just and true, no matter how flawed? We fear this kind of work because it seems to threaten the legitimacy of our own beliefs. I submit that the risk of not reaching out and listening is even greater. As I have insisted, our faith requires us to not be above self-doubt or self-scrutiny. If Christianity cannot understand its own meaning in the context of diversity, it was never very Christian to begin with.

Indeed, one of the most potent notions of Christianity, when accepted at face value, is that God has parental love for all humanity and feels our pains equally, that we are cherished children no matter our religion, nation, culture, language, skin color, sexuality, economic status, and so on. And yet, I think, it is rare that believers really take this to heart. If we did, I suspect politics would indeed change more dramatically than we are prepared for. Wouldn't it change attitudes and policies, especially about oppression in all of its forms, about public health, environmental degradation, war, and poverty? I don't want a politics that feels distinctly Latter-day Saint or Christian. Maybe this seems like heresy, but I say it out of what I consider pretty deep orthodoxy. I want a politics that is so thoroughly Christian that its commitment to the well-being of all people renders it indistinguishable from common decency. No doubt some would call this vision cowardice or a failure to rise to the challenge of my distinctive beliefs. But politics seems to be an arena where good intentions go awry too easily, where implementation can make a mockery of the highest ideals, and where human intentions prove so utterly inadequate to the complexity of our circumstances. Besides, it just does not seem to be the lesson of history that if only we could agree on the same political platform, we would finally have justice, peace, and collective well-being.

So if the goal isn't to achieve the same politics, what is it? It seems it has something to do with being and doing good. And goodness starts with a proper humility. I guess I wonder if it wouldn't necessarily be a bad thing if there were more genuine confusion about politics. I don't mean the confusion that stems from ignorance or apathy. We have far too much of that. I mean the confusion that is generated by an honest and broad approach to problems. The fact that there are many sides to an issue is no reason for apathy or indifference. It only means that we need the courage to engage in dialogue with broad constituencies in order to create the conditions for judicious thinking that can fuel pragmatic solutions to problems. So we need a passionate uncertainty or, to use the phrase invoked earlier, a burning patience that puts us to work with people of different persuasions.

I remember Senator Bill Bradley speaking a generation ago about racial tension in America and urging Americans to be a part of the solution by making friends with people of a different race. He said, "Ask yourself, when was the last time you had a conversation about race with someone of a different race?"[10] This

---

10. Bill Bradley, "Race and Civil Rights in America," speech given at the National Press Club, July 16, 1991.

call is akin to what Krista Tippett has advocated, what she calls "deliberative friendship as political work."[11] I liked the straightforward simplicity of Bradley's argument. Our communities are far too narrow. We associate too often with people who are like us and not enough with people who challenge our assumptions. I think that still holds today not only for race but for tensions between liberals and conservatives, between the rich and the poor, immigrants and citizens, religionists and secularists, town and gown, and so on. Our choices become less meaningful when they are too few and too predictable. Genuine choice is threatened by staid tradition, chauvinism, censorship, and intimidation. Consensus that relies on habitual and categorical trust of some and distrust of others is a threat to the meaning of true community and to freedom itself. Is it too bold to say that freedom *depends* on diversity?

11. "How Friendship and Quiet Conversations Transformed a White Nationalist," *On Being*, May 17, 2018, https://onbeing.org/programs /how-friendship-and-quiet-conversations-transformed-a-white -nationalist-may2018/.

On the Moral Risks
of Reading Scripture

R eading scripture in various religious cultures of the
Book involves risk. If reading is posited as an encounter between the limited human understanding and the
unlimited knowledge of God, faithful reading typically requires
some kind of deference for the pure and transcendent meaning
that the text purports to contain and healthy suspicion toward
the impurities of human perception that might occlude such
meaning. These impurities include our historicity (our embeddedness in time and space) and our partiality (our individual
habits and proclivities of judgment that select and omit idiosyn-
cratically in order to generate our interpretations of experience
and texts alike). There is a rich history of the theology of reading
within various religious traditions that has sought to understand
the dynamics of this human contact with the divine word. It is

This essay was previously published in Joseph M. Spencer and Jenny Webb,
eds., *Reading Nephi Reading Isaiah: 2 Nephi 26–27*, 2nd ed. (Provo, UT: Neal
A. Maxwell Institute for Religious Scholarship, Brigham Young University,
2017); reprinted here with permission.

not my purpose here to rehearse this history but to initiate a conversation, to essay a description of the inherent moral risks of reading implicit in a theology of restoration and continuing revelation. I do so in the hope of avoiding some of the common pitfalls of poor and superficial treatment of the question of what

---

One of the dangers of a believing reader is the confidence that what one understands is *necessarily* divine truth merely because of belief, as if belief alone guarantees the unadulterated truth, untouched by the stains of human perception.

---

it means to read sacred literature. These pitfalls, I insist, are found on both sides of the polarized divide today between the ever-popular secular theories of culture and the entrenched and defensive positions within religious cultures we often find today.

Because the idea of a sacred text inevitably spinning off into infinite meanings, as many literary theories seem to suggest, is a problematic conclusion for believers, it is tempting to insist that a preestablished state of belief is enough to somehow transcend or avoid human dilutions or refractions of the truth. It is perhaps for this reason that believers often spend more religious energy attempting to help others work up the requisite state of belief than thinking about the potential for misunderstanding *within* a state of belief. Certainly one of the dangers of a believing reader is the confidence that what one understands is *necessarily* divine truth merely because of belief, as if belief alone guarantees the unadulterated truth, untouched by the stains of human perception. While such attitudes are not often fully articulated or defended, unfortunately they are often implicitly involved in the formation of belief. And while they are intended to respect the integrity of the sacred text, to the extent that they imagine the exchange between divine will and human understanding as static, they do not seek to account for remainders or gaps in reading. We enter an almost tautological cycle in which, because belief is required for understanding, understanding is identified as an understanding of truth only to the degree that it confirms that prior belief. Right reading here consists of the right belief emerging *before* the reading has even begun to take place; this risks implying, in other words, that reading is unnecessary since it produces nothing new. In this way, reading is imagined in such a way as to avoid the moral risk of judgment. Even a brief consideration of the political and sectarian dogmatism within many religious cultures today—and the concomittant neglect of the rich complexity of their own sacred texts—provides enough evidence that such reading theologies are alive and well.

The notion that belief precedes understanding stands opposed to the commonplace secular view of literature that has predominated in secular culture at least since Nietzsche's declaration of the death of God. In this view, judgment tends to take precedence over belief, and certainly over any notion of inspiration or revelation. According to Giles Gunn, in modern secular reading practices "one reinterprets for the sake of believing once again in the possibility of understanding and thereby rediscovers what it is like to believe."[1] Such attitudes respect the autonomy of the reader and her capacity to produce new understandings while bypassing the problem posed by the possibility of divine

---

1. Giles Gunn, *The Interpretation of Otherness: Literature, Religion, and the American Imagination* (New York: Oxford University Press, 1979), 47–48.

intervention and communication of meaning. The implication, in other words, is that reading produces perpetually diversified meanings or "truths" that are merely idiosyncratic for each reader but never transcendent. Curiously here again, the reader evades moral risk since what is sought is merely an interpretation that holds a certain kind of creative integrity, persuasiveness, or style. Not surprisingly, we have seen over the course of the past century an increasing distance between these two positions, placing secular and sacred literature at greater and greater distance from one another because of the fundamental and mistaken assumption that they require irreconcilable reading strategies.

I wish to suggest that as a modern-day book of divine origin and translation, the Book of Mormon collapses this binary opposition between sacred and secular reading practices. It is a book of scripture that offers transcendent understanding in response to individual belief, but because the understanding that it offers reminds us constantly of the inevitability of remainders, it also offers grounds for belief in ultimacy. In its perpetual metatextual reminders about the inherent textuality of understanding, as well as the need for abridgment, revision, rephrasing, appropriation, and the seeming inevitability of anachronism (things that Nephi's use of Isaiah and other biblical language demonstrates particularly well), the Book of Mormon highlights the dynamic and incomplete nature of interpretation. In this sense it raises the moral stakes—both the costs and the benefits—of reading, forcefully foregrounding the need to bring ourselves fully to the text, rather than emptying ourselves of all prejudice and partiality, and the need to revise and to rethink what we thought we believed. The Book of Mormon demonstrates the paradox that no transcendent meaning can be gleaned from it without at least some individual wager of belief as to what it might mean. Indeed, all *transcendent* meaning appears to be dependent on the bets of the *contingent* reader. It thus raises the moral stakes of reading to insist simultaneously on the divine and omniscient ultimacy that lies behind words to which we are answerable as well as on the need for creative, idiosyncratic readings that stem from the particulars and impurities of our historical and partial conditions as individual human readers. As the emblem of a theology of continual revelation, the Book of Mormon also sheds important light on the not-so-different processes of interpreting sacred and secular texts. In what follows, I wish to explore the theological implications of this process before turning to a passage in 2 Nephi where we can identify these tensions.

TOWARD MUTUALITY

Matthew Arnold could never have argued for the inherent value of great works of literature in an environment that did not see texts themselves as primary determinants of meaning.[2] The very humanism he inherited from at least the Renaissance suggested that great books shape and mold great minds, great citizens, moral people. But in the West's disillusion with this "you are what you read" formula, we began to assume a Nietzschean responsibility to be more accountable for the worlds of our own making: it was not so much the text as the proactive creativity of the reader that could or should make meaning. In contemporary criticism we are beginning to see a turning away from the polarizations implied in these two positions, coupled with a yearning for some way to reconcile these two (valid) views—a yearning that provides an opening for rethinking the nature of sacred literature.

Certainly, without attention to the shifting patterns of reading in culture, we become blind to the ways we want to read particular meanings into texts, and it is not difficult to see the

---

2. Matthew Arnold, *Culture and Anarchy* (New York: Oxford World's Classics, 2009).

danger in that. On the other hand, without due attention to the text itself, we render all literature and all readings of equal value, something with which any believer in an authoritative text will inevitably feel uncomfortable. When this kind of radical flattening of the horizon of literary distinction occurs—between greater and lesser works of literature, between a poem, an essay, and a newspaper article, as we see in some forms of New Historicism or reader-response theory, for example—it also becomes virtually impossible to argue for the importance of the distinction between sacred and secular literature. And as I have suggested, one way of ensuring that the text receives its due attention is to assert that scripture itself assumes priority as determinative of its meaning and truthfulness, such that the truth of the word of God would seem to be self-contained and in no need of any reader's agency, historicity, or prejudice. If this attitude becomes excessive in its defensiveness, however, it begins to be intolerant of the ways in which the contingency of the human reader can become entangled or commingled with the will and mind of God. Human agency is assumed to contaminate and divert, perhaps even to pervert, the ways of God in the minds of men. And indeed Peter, who warns that scripture is by definition not "of any private interpretation" (2 Peter 1:20),[3] also warns against the self-destruction of such misinterpretation. Speaking of Paul's epistles, he notes:

> As also in all his epistles, speaking in them of these things; in which are some things hard to be understood, which they that are unlearned and unstable wrest, as they do also the other scriptures, unto their own destruction. Ye therefore, beloved, seeing ye know

---

3. Note, of course, that the standard approach to 2 Peter 1:20 is heavy-handed. Commentators generally agree that the passage has reference to the prophet's interpretation of his or her revelatory experience, not to the reader's interpretation of scripture.

these things before, beware lest ye also, being led away with the error of the wicked, fall from your own stedfastness. But grow in grace, and in the knowledge of our Lord and Saviour Jesus Christ. To him be glory both now and for ever. Amen. (2 Peter 3:16–18)

Or as Alma simply says in the Book of Mormon, "Behold, the scriptures are before you; if ye will wrest them it shall be to your own destruction" (Alma 13:20).[4]

These are strong warnings. But, as my reading of 2 Nephi will show, they do not need to imply that we cannot bring our per-

---

There is an essential moral weakness in the tendency to avoid confronting the human stains within sacred literature, just as there is in a hermeneutics of suspicion that distrusts its revelatory claims.

---

sonality and invest it in the reading experience. If the refreshing and renewing power of new readers is disallowed, we may find ourselves leaning too heavily on the crutches of tradition and habit (and not, ironically, on the text), making ourselves vulnerable to assuming that language perpetually generates the same meanings across all times and places. We would, in other words,

---

4. Note that to be learned, in these texts, is not to have profound knowledge of language or history or to have exegetical prowess, but to repent and submit oneself to grace and belief in Christ so that proper understanding can be granted.

have to concede that human agency, imagination, and experience play no role whatsoever in the generation of divine meaning. While this would protect and keep unambiguously clear the boundaries between the human and the divine, such reliance on tradition actually bypasses rather than protects the special truthfulness of God's word. In order to preserve the notion of the text's special status above and beyond human stains, this approach holds to the promise of an absolute and transcendently correct reading, a mastery of the text. As Alan Jacobs argues, this position of mastery easily slides into a categorical suspicion of and freedom from the text and thus is not invested in the moral risks of reading. Though "'freedom from' and 'mastery of' are related but not identical concepts," he points out, each entails "the elimination . . . of an ongoing dialogical encounter with the text, in which the reader and the text subject each other to scrutiny. . . . In neither case is there anything like real reverence, love, or friendship—in Bakhtin's term, *faithfulness* is lacking—and thus, in neither case is the readerly/critical experience productive of genuine knowledge (of the self or the other)."[5]

There is an essential moral weakness in the tendency to avoid confronting the human stains within sacred literature, just as there is in a hermeneutics of suspicion that distrusts its revelatory claims. In both cases the reader is never required to take what Jacobs calls the "enormous risks" of using discernment.[6] In the former case, to assume a radical textual determinism is to assume it is merely and always the text that produces meaning, never the reader. The inherent risk of engaging one's agency, choices, and judgment as a reader is bypassed in the interest of a meaning that is simply given, though how and why it is given or not given are rarely explained or are poorly theorized. Acts of

---

5. Alan Jacobs, *A Theology of Reading: The Hermeneutics of Love* (Boulder, CO: Westview Press, 2001), 70.
6. Jacobs, *Theology of Reading*, 88.

interpretation in such a model are ultimately self-delusions since the agency involved in discernment is ignored: a reader strictly intolerant of the ambiguities of human perceptions of divine will cannot explain how she avoids worshipping a god after her own image. In the case of a hermeneutics of suspicion, on the other hand, the determinism tends to lie with the reader who produces all meaning, the text being radically excluded from the process of meaning-making. The inherent risk of being answerable to an authority or a source of knowledge outside oneself is bypassed in the interest of a meaning that is simply chosen. Acts of interpretation in such a model are ultimately solipsistic illusions because the agency of discernment is the only agency at work: a reader strictly intolerant of the possibility of divine intervention and communication cannot explain how she avoids the false consciousness she originally sets out to escape.

There is, however, another possibility, one that seeks what the theologian Reinhold Niebuhr calls "mutuality."[7] Great knowledge comes at great risk—what Paul Ricoeur calls the very "wager" at the heart of all interpretation[8]—and one of the risks of reading scripture is to bet on one's interpretive capacity to discern the will of God. To have faith is to believe in the possibility that a mingling of human and divine understanding does not have to lead to deception even if it also means abdicating the need for absolute certainty. Faith maintains a margin of freedom from the text even as it seeks communion and understanding. Jacobs compares this mutuality to the dialogic imagination of Bakhtin, a kind of hope in a fruitful give-and-take between the reader and the text. He explains: "This hope involves neither *demand* nor *expectation*; indeed, if it demanded or expected it would not be hope."[9] Thus while "absolute suspicion—one that

---

7. Jacobs, *Theology of Reading*, 88.
8. Jacobs, *Theology of Reading*, 88.
9. Jacobs, *Theology of Reading*, 89; emphasis in original.

always and on principle refuses Ricoeur's wager—is the natural outworking of despair," its apparent opposite of "triumphalist confidence" (the "presumption" that one has apprehended truth that is always transcendently and eternally unchangeable) is also a form of "hopelessness."[10]

I would suggest that the mutuality toward which Jacobs gestures can be heard in the Lord's chastisement in the first section of the Doctrine and Covenants. While the Lord criticizes those who "seek not the Lord to establish his righteousness" because every one of them "walketh in his own way, and after the image of his own god, whose image is in the likeness of the world, and whose substance is that of an idol" (Doctrine and Covenants 1:16), we learn that it is precisely our human tendency to imagine gods and worlds of our own making that the Lord requires in order to reveal *his* will to us through his prophets, so that we might be corrected and gain wisdom. God's dilemma thus is that he must speak to his servants "in their weakness, after the manner of their language" (v. 24). This mutuality of God's language and human language, between God's omniscience and our limited imagination, makes up the very structure of continuing revelation.

So what are the moral risks of reading scripture if we embrace the model of mutuality? We risk self-deluding idol worship—worshipping the god of our imagination—on one hand, and we risk self-exposure to the piercing eye of God on the other. There is no escape from these risks. We must be willing also to admit we have been wrong—wrong about God and wrong about ourselves. We must risk, in other words, the possibility of error because that is the only way we might learn precisely where, in fact, we have erred. We generally do not take such risks unless we are willing to wager that such knowledge will change us, heal

---

10. Jacobs, *Theology of Reading*, 89.

us, draw us closer to godliness. There is, on the one hand, error that leads to destruction, as Peter remarks (see 2 Peter 3:16), but there is, on the other, what the atonement makes of the errors we bring to the Lord: he turns the weaknesses and conditions of our human existence into the necessary stepping stones—the strengths of our sanctification.

By asking us consistently to liken its pages to ourselves, as well as by consistently demonstrating through allegorical representation the risks and rewards of our interpretations, the Book of Mormon opens itself up perpetually to the contemporary moment of its reader. It makes actual its claims each and every time it is read. In this sense, for all its divinity, the Book of Mormon is also literally always secular—a word that indicates, among other things, that something is "in human time." The book, in other words, embodies the paradox that God spoke and continues to speak "in human time," that prophets wrote and continue to write in human language, and that our reading practices cannot eschew—either through triumphalist confidence in received tradition or through secular despair in the face of the sacred—the inherent answerability and mutuality of the act of reading.

SYMBOLISM AND THE SACRED

To this point, I have been speaking at a relatively abstract or theoretical level. Is there anything in scriptural texts themselves that justifies what I have outlined above regarding the nature of reading scripture? In the remainder of this essay, I would like to argue that there are, perhaps particularly in the Book of Mormon, consistent indications that reading scripture must take the kind of mutuality I have described as its aim. My argument, though, will not be that scripture makes an explicit claim about reading at the level of *content*, but rather that its very manner of inscription and internal organization implicitly gestures in the direction of a reading *process* of mutuality.

If we are to push the implications of the Doctrine and Covenants passage cited above, all forms of revelation in sacred literature are translations between divinity and humanity, and it is therefore no accident that we find in books that make special claims about points of contact between the human and the divine such a high level of figurative language, indirection, and self-reflexive metatextuality. Instead of signifying their fictionality, however, these symbols exhibit an inherent respect for and anticipation of the human reception of divine revelation that is built into the very structure of sacred texts. Thus, despite their didactic style and often declarative and imperative tense, scriptures also exhibit what Ricoeur calls their own "interpretive dynamism": "the text interprets before having been interpreted."[11]

This is an important feature of sacred texts that is often ignored by believing and nonbelieving readers alike. Figurative language implicitly, if not explicitly, acknowledges the text's own partiality and its dependence on readers for the text to expand and magnify its meaning and thereby to work out its potential universality. Ricoeur points both to the sacred text's capacity to imagine its own poetic force and to the consequent need for a semiotic approach (as opposed to a "historical-critical method"). Understanding the truths of revelation is not so much a matter of contextual scholarship or even specialized exegesis, but a measured response to the guidance of the text's internally organized symbolism. Revelation, for Ricoeur, is thus the moment of transfer from the seemingly ahistorical space of a sacred meaning into our own history, something akin to what Nephi describes when

---

11. Paul Ricoeur, *Figuring the Sacred: Religion, Narrative, and Imagination*, trans. David Pellauer, ed. Mark I. Wallace (Minneapolis, MN: Fortress Press, 1995), 161.

he asks us to "liken" the scriptures to ourselves (1 Nephi 19:23). Readerly imagination displaces or relocates the text's meaning in the reader's capacity to imagine the figural nature of the text. Ricoeur explains: "A meaning potential in the language—that is, in the things already said—is liberated through the entangled twofold process of metaphorizing the narrative and narrativizing the metaphor."[12]

What Ricoeur describes here is a kind of dialogue between a dynamic, receptive, and changeable reader and a dynamic, receptive, and changeable text. Belief in the possibility of the former—which is belief in the possibility of repentance and of the atonement itself—necessitates belief in the latter.[13] Ricoeur insists, in other words, that if there is a readerly need to metaphorize the narrative of a sacred text, that need itself arises (as a response) from a semiotic pattern, already established within the text, that narrativizes metaphors. He takes as an example the parable of the sower, in which the "destiny of the sowing is metaphorized as the destiny of the word, [and] the destiny of the word is narrativized as the destiny of the sowing."[14] The sacred text, in other words, inserts "into the meaning of what is said something about its being said and its reception."[15]

---

12. Ricoeur, *Figuring the Sacred*, 159. Of course, there is no way to know for sure that one's wager on the meaningfulness of scriptural symbols will always bear fruit, but without the risk of feeling after this meaningfulness there can never be any corroborating response to the metatextual clues of the text. In the end, all declarations regarding the meaning of revelation will merely and always be grounded in misreadings, and all claims regarding the inherent secular nature of *all* literary forms will be justified.

13. The perhaps ironic implication is that a fundamentalist notion of a sacred and unchanging, once-revealed Word is counterproductive, barring human change.

14. Ricoeur, *Figuring the Sacred*, 159.

15. Ricoeur, *Figuring the Sacred*, 158.

If we were similarly to consider Lehi's journey into the wilderness, we would say that the story appears to have metaphorical shape, that it can be read as a metaphor for the mortal journey to the promised land of heaven. Certainly this is not an uncommon reading of the narrative, for we hear countless attempts in talks, lessons, and sermons to identify the liahonas in our lives, the Lamans and Lemuels, the trials of broken bows, and so on. What

> The Book of Mormon seems to insist rather emphatically on its textuality, making clear that reading, abridging, editing, and translating are integral components of being a seer who is also a translator.

is striking in the narrative, however, is how often this metaphorizing—and this is to Ricoeur's point—is anticipated *in the narrative itself*. We see, for example, that the Book of Mormon is at pains to let us know that Lehi's stories and dreams are all told to us only secondhand by his son Nephi (whose recounting is inevitably mediated by his receiving learning in the language of his fathers) and only after having passed through the editorial hand of Mormon—and we, of course, can read these heavily mediated narratives only in the translation provided by Joseph Smith. The book seems to insist rather emphatically on its textuality, making clear that reading, abridging, editing, and translating are integral components of being a seer who is also a translator.

But let us turn to a shorter, more specific text in order to illustrate this point more fully. Nephi's frequent and extensive borrowing from the language of Isaiah exemplifies the prophetic editorial work I have just described. The text tells us that Nephi is a close reader of texts but that he sees in the language of prophecy and revelation an opportunity to add likening layers of meaning that allow for multiple contexts and contingent readings that are still faithful to the mind and will of God. This is one of the Book of Mormon's most important and provocative ideas, and it implicitly suggests that faithful reading should be generous, aware but forgiving of human stains and weakness in the work of giving new life to the otherwise dead letter, just as God appears to be willing and able to use the same limited human language across a variety of contexts without compromising his truths. In fact, the implication seems to be that God's transcendent and revealed meaning actually *depends on* multiple readings in order to reveal the fullness of his truth, which is to say that the truth depends on human imagination, one reader at a time. Seeing multiple applications for the same passages of scripture to radically distinct moments in human history, Nephi encourages us to do the same.

In perhaps one of the most important instances of Nephi's approach to Isaiah, we see in 2 Nephi 27 a citation of verses from Isaiah 29 alluding to a sealed book that cannot be read. That the passage appears to be a prophecy of our time would seem to be the reason for its citation, but it comes to us as such only because it is, as presented in the text, already interpreted by Nephi. Nephi's editorial work here is a reading we are asked to model, and it is a perfect example of what Ricoeur means by suggesting that we should metaphorize narrative (creatively read 2 Nephi 27), which is already a narrativized metaphor (2 Nephi 27 being already a creative reading of Isaiah 29). When we are told that this book contains the words of "those who have slumbered in the dust" and that they shall be delivered "unto another" (2 Nephi 27:9), we are presented with a reference to the words of the dead that are, among other possibilities, an emblem of the book—the Book of Mormon—in our hands.

Of course, we know that this is a prophecy of the Book of Mormon at least because of the Charles Anthon incident. It would be a narrow reading, however, to see it only as a prophecy of this particular incident and therefore only as a prophecy about the Book of Mormon. Admittedly, the language of the prophecy points us in this direction. Note, for example, just how much more detail is provided in Nephi's version of Isaiah's text than in the Bible, detail that seems clearly intended to secure the connection with the Anthon incident. But Nephi expands on the story enough to go through specification to a kind of generalization. For example, 2 Nephi 27:6 establishes simply that the Lord will bring forth unto his addressee ("unto you") the words of a book that will come from them who have slumbered. But Nephi appears to be addressing the remnant of the house of Israel as well as all people everywhere, especially those who have "closed [their] eyes" and "rejected the prophets" because of iniquity (v. 5). So it is a historically specific people of the covenant he addresses (the remnant of the house of Israel), but also apparently any generic reader whatsoever.[16] Thus, even as he adds details to Isaiah's text in order to secure a connection between the prophecy of Isaiah and the Anthon incident, Nephi himself begins to allegorize that latter-day incident, providing the beginnings of its universalization.

16. This is surmised from Nephi's opening address in this chapter to the Jews and the Gentiles and to "those who shall be upon other lands, yea, even upon all the lands of the earth" (2 Nephi 27:1).

Importantly, Nephi's implicit allegorization of the Anthon incident is anticipated in the allegorizing language of Isaiah himself. Note that Isaiah speaks allegorically when he says, "The vision of all is become unto you *as* the words of a book that is sealed" (Isaiah 29:11; emphasis added). It is this *as* into which Nephi inserts his own creative appropriation of Isaiah 29. And Nephi's explanations, the context of nineteenth-century experience, and our own contemporary perspective would seem to complete the allegory: the rejection of the authenticated translation by a learned man is an allegory of the wisdom of the world more generally and its rejection of revelation—a mistake we must not make. Going still further, though, one can take as allegorical also the sacred book in 2 Nephi 27, understanding it as an emblem of a history—*any* history—that is lost to us until sufficient repentance has taken place. The reader, on this approach, is implied to be someone always awaiting the further opening of a sealed book. Indeed, because the Book of Mormon itself makes note of its own sealed and lost portions and makes claims about other records yet to come forth until all revelations (i.e., Isaiah's "vision of all" or Nephi's "revelation from God, from the beginning of the world to the ending thereof," 2 Nephi 27:7) are finally read, it (the Book of Mormon itself) can serve only as an intermediate step, a stepping-stone, as it were, toward a greater understanding of God's revelations. Even as it reveals, the book in Isaiah's/Nephi's prophecy keeps us aware of the still-slumbering dead, of ourselves as perhaps the still-slumbering reader, and of every sealed book still awaiting further translation.

Verses 10 and 11 of 2 Nephi 27, moreover, seem to clarify the distinction between two kinds of sealed books and aid us in understanding this idea. One book is sealed because of pride, wickedness, and wisdom of the world. This is the portion of the book described as given to "another,"[17] but it is distinct from the sealed book that holds "all things from the foundation of the world unto the end thereof" (v. 10). One way of understanding this might be to suggest that there is wickedness that prevents some from accepting the divinity of the Book of Mormon, and there is wickedness endemic to the human condition as such that prevents all of us—even those who accept the Book of Mormon—from being ready to "read by the power of Christ" to the point that "all things shall be revealed until the children of men which ever have been among the children of men" (v. 11). Can we assume that as long as history remains a mystery to us—as long as all we can produce is fragmented knowledge—it is a sign that we remain in this general state of insufficient grace in order to be able to read the meaning of all things? Certainly, we are here implicitly enjoined to retain hope and resist the temptations of both secular chauvinism and the believer's triumphalist confidence that Nephi chastises in later chapters when he complains of those who proclaim, "All is well! . . . We have got a Bible!" (2 Nephi 28:21, 25; 29:3–13).

Verse 12 adds an interesting twist to all this. The verse declares that when the book is delivered to "the man of whom I have spoken" (surely Joseph Smith), "the book shall be hid from the eyes of the world." Such hiding was earlier spoken of in somewhat more allegorical terms (the slumbering, blind, and dreaming wicked who cannot understand God's revelations), but here it seems both allegorical *and* literal: "the eyes of none shall behold it save it be that three witnesses shall behold it." What seems especially rich about this figural and literal blindness, this figural and literal revelation, is that it posits the possibility that the very dichotomy between figural and literal is false. A refusal

---

17. The footnote for verse 10 in the 1981 edition of the Book of Mormon sends the reader to Joseph Smith—History 1:65, the story of the Anthon incident.

to read a sealed book, on the one hand, is here contrasted with the blessing of seeing the physical plates. The former position is based on faith in rationalism to the point that it refuses empirical evidence, the latter on faith in revelation to the point that it is rewarded with empirical evidence. The authentication of the translation, in other words, will not come from worldly wisdom but from, of all things, empirical experience, albeit facilitated and supplemented "by the power of God." The Book of Mormon, although suggestive of God's many mysteries, is not shrouded in mysticism. It is a book that promises revelation and delivers on

---

The Book of Mormon, although suggestive of God's many mysteries, is not shrouded in mysticism. It is a book that promises revelation and delivers on its promise to those willing to make the wager.

---

its promise to those willing to make the wager. Unwillingness leads to our own condemnation—the only and very important caveat being that we should be careful not to overstate what we know, since the book in our hands is a metonym of the great book recording all things from the foundation of the world, a book that remains at least partly if not still substantially sealed.

Thus the sealed book in Isaiah becomes a prophecy about something much more fundamental and widely applicable than just an instantiation of the Book of Mormon's historicity and truthfulness. It is a prophecy about prophecy, a revelation about revelation, and it reaches from the beginning to the end of time.

The sealed book is an emblem of the very language and knowledge of God and of our relationship to the hope we may or may not have in God's capacity to reveal all things to us. This would suggest that obtaining the power to revive the meaning of the words of the dead requires something from the reader: a purification of the heart, a point verse 12 makes most emphatically. Such purification does not happen, though, without our wagering on the possibility that a sealed book can speak, nor without risking the possibility that what it speaks might reveal the fullness of our sins and wickedness. No one wants to open such a Pandora's box without the hope that such knowledge will cleanse and purify: it damns *only* the one unwilling to believe it can be read or, as it were, unsealed. The sealed book in Isaiah and Nephi is therefore an emblem of hope in our potential, ultimately, to know all things, to obtain the mind of God. In this sense it is also a warning of what we stand to lose when we assume the "learned" arrogance of a hermeneutics of suspicion, or when we assume the triumphalist confidence that we have all we need, that we have indeed already taken possession of the mind of God by virtue of having obtained a fundamental knowledge of his revelations.

Ricoeur insists that a "a theology that confronts the inevitability of the divine plan with the refractory nature of human actions and passions is a theology that engenders narrative."[18] Surely a theology like ours that produces texts and narratives in excess of the Bible is guilty as charged: it insists on this meeting ground between a divine plan and the unpredictable and potentially chaotic nature of multiple, individual interpretations. Consistent, then, with the fundamental meaning of a God in mortal flesh, it insists that the sacred is an encounter between the will of God and the will of human beings, the language

---

18. Ricoeur, *Figuring the Sacred*, 182.

of God and the language of human beings, heaven and earth, spirit and body. In so doing, our theology perpetually produces texts that, in their overt textuality, suggest their own nature as palimpsests and therefore point to the need for the poetic imagination of readers and the unending need for more readers to come. What in other words keeps scripture alive and dynamic and from becoming flattened out by the exercises of tradition is the vivification of new interpretations, which is another way of saying that what makes the gospel true is its relevance to human narratives, seized upon by one reader at a time.

Rising to the challenge of reading revealed words seems, in a word, to begin with a paradoxical recognition of the fact of the Lord's having withheld the fullness of revelation from us, of the fact that what we are reading in scripture is always partial, incomplete, and stained by human weakness. This opens up for the reader a choice: either I want to know all things, *even if it means I must confess that I have erred and will continue to err in my quest to love God and gain his knowledge*; or I do not want to know all things, *even if it means that in my fear I err*. It is a choice literally between life and death. We are broken, wayward humans either way. But the hope in Christ is hope in a translation that miraculously places the will and mind of God in human flesh and posits the hope of such dead flesh finally conforming to the life-giving will and mind of God, a resurrection of the mind, as it were. To read scripture in faith is, in the end, to believe in the possibility that all our broken readings might somehow be made whole once all the pages of the sealed book have finally been opened.

Reading and the Menardian Paradox in 3 Nephi

I n the Old World, Jesus taught, "Blessed are they which do hunger and thirst after righteousness: for they shall be filled" (Matthew 5:6), and yet in the New World he says, "Blessed are all they who do hunger and thirst after righteousness, for they shall be filled with the Holy Ghost" (3 Nephi 12:6). Attention, understandably, has been given to the differences large and small between the Sermon on the Mount as recounted in the New Testament and the similar sermon given in the New World. At times we note slight shifts in emphasis (here in the New World Jesus makes this promise to "all," as if to place extra emphasis), perhaps more complete understandings (we are filled with something quite particular, the gift of the Holy Ghost as the promised comforter), and so on. And these differences raise compelling questions about the possibility of those plain and precious truths that were lost in translation in the Bible but are restored again in the Book of Mormon. Or perhaps the differences suggest a

This essay was previously published in *Journal of Book of Mormon Studies* 26 (2017): 165–84; reprinted here with permission.

shifting context, a telling response on the part of Jesus to his different circumstances that might have justified slight variations in the speech. Or perhaps it undermines the very idea of a set speech or script.

But there is an additional question that the two accounts of Christ's sermon raise. What of the fact that in most cases the wording is exactly coincident? What might that signify? Jesus tells his listeners in the Old World, "Blessed are the merciful: for they shall obtain mercy" (Matthew 5:7). He tells his audience in the New World, "Blessed are the merciful, for they shall obtain mercy" (3 Nephi 12:7). The punctuational difference aside, are we to assume a meaning that is precisely coincident in both contexts? Might the same language spoken in different places and in a different moment in time necessarily shift in meaning? What, in any case, are we to make of the fact that both statements in standard King James English are not the original language spoken in either case, and that the two original languages are dramatically different? What does the occasional overlap and coincidence with the Bible in the Book of Mormon ask of us exactly?

Here I focus on the repetition of the Sermon on the Mount in 3 Nephi in order to offer a literary and theological reflection on the Book of Mormon itself. My question concerns not the content of the sermon so much as the moral stakes of reading scripture, and especially of reading Latter-day Saint scripture, which I take to be scripture that places special emphasis on its own weaknesses, textuality, and constructedness. Taking as my companion Jorge Luis Borges, I argue that these features that exercise both the Book of Mormon's defenders and its attackers are necessary to the theological meaning of the text rather than difficulties that need to be explained and that they highlight an essential meaning of the act of reading scripture germane to a theology of continuing revelation.

PIERRE MENARD AND SCRIPTURE

The great Argentine author Jorge Luis Borges wrote what may be his most famous short story, "Pierre Menard, Author of the *Quixote*," in 1939 to restore an understanding of the central paradox of what it means to read. The story is a mock scholarly article about a fictional early twentieth-century French writer by the name of Pierre Menard.[1] Lost among Menard's many accomplishments, claims the fictional scholar, are fragments of an attempt to write *Don Quixote*, the novel already written by the great seventeenth-century Spanish author Miguel de Cervantes. The narrator clarifies this was not an attempt to put the character of Don Quixote in modern garb, like some modern adaptation of Romeo and Juliet set in Los Angeles. Adaptions merely "produce the plebeian pleasure of anachronism or (what is worse) . . . enthrall us with the elementary idea that all epochs are the same or are different."[2] Instead, Menard's project was to do something quite different—something seemingly impossible.

I will come back to that impossible task in a moment. First, I want to highlight here Borges's hesitation in deciding whether anachronism signals that all epochs are the same or whether it signals that all epochs are different. I want to suggest that this conundrum is central to understanding not only Borges's story but also what it might mean to read scripture. I insist that the question of how historical, geographical, and cultural contexts shape the way we write and read is ultimately undecidable, even though those contexts are undeniably relevant to how we arrive at understandings of textual meaning. Let me explain. On one hand, we might be tempted to emphasize context, as the onetime

---

1. Jorge Luis Borges, *Labyrinths: Selected Stories and Other Writings* (New York: New Directions, 1964), 36–44.
2. Borges, *Labyrinths*, 39.

school of reader-response theory did, and insist that all readings are produced primarily or even solely by the context of the reader. To do so is to insist on the radical and perpetual *difference* between any two given moments in time and any two readers. But for Borges, this point is obvious and even boring. There is no denying that the reader's situation shapes a text's meaning

---

According to the prophets, interpretation of scripture is a moral act— we might get it right and we might get it woefully wrong. Indeed, we will be judged by the books God has given us.

---

according to her needs and desires, but if we can't distinguish between a good and bad reading, we must concede that all readings are misreadings and are equally off target. If this were the case, why would we want to insist on the difference, for example, between wresting the scriptures and likening them to ourselves? According to the prophets, interpretation of scripture is a moral act—we might get it right and we might get it woefully wrong. Indeed, we will be judged by the books God has given us. And if meaning were *merely* produced by readerly context, then there would be no possibility of transcendent value in texts—let alone, in the case of scripture, of any revelation from God to human beings. Texts would mean only what people think they mean, and all people would have equal claim on interpretation, regardless of the text. Hence, to reduce a text's meaning merely to its various interpretations in the hands of its thousands of readers is to render all textual meaning and all texts equal under the omnipotent and unbending law of context. Scripture would then hold no special privilege over any other kind of literature, be it a magazine advertisement or a novel by William Faulkner. On such a view, the only way to enrich reading would be to be aware of our own historical entrapment as readers. As readers we would have the critical obligation to historicize and secularize everything, paying attention solely to the subtle and subconscious ways in which all readers—ourselves included—hide their willful interpretations under the guise of transcendent meaning.

So it would initially seem that if we are invested in a belief in the special nature of scripture, as is presumably the case with any believing reader of the Book of Mormon, we must resist reader-response theory categorically. But, of course, to insist instead that meaning is always contained solely in the text itself, or that it is no more or no less than the author's intentions, is to slide into the other extreme rejected by Borges, according to which all epochs are indeed the same. If all epochs and all cultures are the same, why should we need new revelations? Such a position disregards all the ways in which language, culture, historical experience, and beliefs shape and guide the kinds of questions we as readers or writers bring to texts. And this places our own judgment beyond reproach by denying the relevance of our moment and place in a culture and in historical time. Such a philosophy of reading seems almost ashamed of our humanity and places hope in scripture as a categorical escape from it. It is not surprising that such attitudes are often accompanied by a general suspicion of or lack of interest in all forms of secular literature, even the "best books" we are told we ought to seek out, since they cannot offer a similar power of escape (Doctrine and Covenants 88:118). Thus, in an effort to save scripture from the claims of reader-response theory, we might end up mistakenly insisting on an exceptional view of sacred writ and drawing an overly firm line between the divine word and human will. Fundamentalists and relativists alike find a belief in the similarities between literature and scripture threatening since such a belief threatens to confuse categories of values essential for their respective projects of interpretation.

I want to insist, with Borges, that at both extremes—one we might call radically fundamentalist and the other radically relativist—we create an untraversable abyss between the sacred and the secular, leaving us mistakenly self-assured that we see a radical (and essentially knowable) distinction between that which comes from God and that which comes from human beings. I would argue that such a sharp dichotomy between the timeless and the timely is unacceptable from the perspective of Latter-day Saint theology, a theology that insists on the need for continuing revelation, on more prophets and more books yet to come from peoples and cultures who have not yet joined the chorus of testimonies we have thus far heard. We might call Latter-day Saint theology *dynamically orthodox*. We adhere to what we have received not out of fear of competition but in anticipation of what is yet to be revealed.

Let's return to the passage from Borges to see if it might enlighten us further. His narrator explains that Menard's task differs from what these extremes represent. Menard's goal, it turns out, is not to produce another *Quixote*, "but *the Quixote itself*. Needless to say, he never contemplated a mechanical transcription of the original; he did not propose to copy it. His admirable intention was to produce a few pages which would coincide—word for word and line for line—with those of Miguel de Cervantes."[3] Menard himself thinks of this task, so much more interesting than the task of producing mere anachronism or inhabiting either of the extremes criticized above, as akin to

---

3.   Borges, *Labyrinths*, 39.

the work of metaphysicians who labor to produce an indisputable affirmation of a transcendent truth, except that in his case there will be no publication of the "intermediary stages" of his labor. All Menard can offer to the world is his text as final proof of the mysterious process by which he was able to produce the same words. At first he thinks he can accomplish his aims simply by trying to *be Cervantes*, but then he realizes that the real challenge would be to produce such coincidence in language *as Pierre Menard*—to find the meeting ground between his world and the world of Cervantes through a production of identical words. Even though it appears he was successful in producing at least part of the same text, the fictional scholar and narrator points out the irony that the perfect coincidence between the *words* produced by Menard and the words originally produced by Cervantes highlights only their very different *meanings*, since the words are produced in radically different contexts. The narrator cites two identical passages, one from Cervantes and the other from Menard, and concludes that the passage produced by Menard is full of greater irony and meaning! His reasoning? It cannot be for nothing that three centuries of Western history have transpired between Cervantes and Menard. The same words will reverberate as different meanings only because of the considerable changes of time and place that shape how those words are interpreted.

The Menardian paradox is therefore that the achievement of coincidence and sameness of language—an achievement that has relied on an extraordinary level of devotion to and not mere mechanical reproduction of the original text—not only doesn't escape the difference of context but in fact highlights it in order to produce new meaning. What Borges's short story underscores in its rhetorical position as an academic article is "the halting and rudimentary art of reading: this new technique is that of the deliberate anachronism and the erroneous attribution."[4] Menard's ambition might be a possibility only in the realm of ironic fiction, yet it is certainly what happens every time a reader picks up a text. Reading enacts an exact coincidence of language between the written word and the read word, especially when it is read carefully and devotedly; the same words echo in the mind

> The text is the catalyst that spurs all readers to become cocreators of the text's meaning and value. Truth needs a revelator as much as it needs a translator or interpreter.

of a writer and of a reader no matter how many centuries might have transpired in the meantime (unless of course it is a translation, but Borges insists that reading is translation in any case, as we will see). Because reading always produces new meanings, reading always makes of the text, as the narrator points out is the case with Menard's *Quixote*, "a kind of palimpsest" in which the traces of earlier readings are faintly visible on the text.[5] In the Borgesian universe, the reader becomes aware of the impossibility of plumbing the depths of a text to the point of arriving at ground zero of the word's origin. All readings are rereadings, translations, as are all writings. That is, every reader has left her mark on the text—every reading a new rewriting of earlier layers—which blurs the distinction between author and reader.

---

4.   Borges, *Labyrinths*, 44.
5.   Borges, *Labyrinths*, 44.

For this reason Borges once wrote in a preface to a book of his own poems, "If the pages of this book contain some well-crafted verse, may the reader forgive my daring in having composed it before him. We are all one; our trifles are of little import, and circumstances influence our souls to such a degree that it is almost a chance occurrence that you are the reader and I the writer—the diffident and zealous writer—of my verses."[6] Far from creating a universe of relativism, this stunning disavowal of the notion of authenticity and originality places the transcendent value and meaning of the text beyond the individual reach of the author and any one reader. If it bothers us to have to demystify an author's "genius" in this way, it also grants us hope that we too as readers have the opportunity, even the responsibility, to be coparticipants, co-creators of genius or transcendent meaning. Untouched by genius or by holiness, the reader can scarcely perceive genius or identify revelation in another. The text is the catalyst that spurs all readers to become co-creators of the text's meaning and value. This implies that "the creative process is essentially a reading" and therefore that "only through an act of interpretation can that which is postulated take on meaning."[7] Truth needs a revelator as much as it needs a translator or interpreter. And this creative process happens both at the moment of creation as well as in the moment of reading, according to Borges. Hence, "meaning develops from the twofold relation of the interpreter: to a literary dream world *and* to historical context."[8]

All of this, of course, bears on scripture. When we consider divine meaning, revealed from God to human beings, we might feel tempted to conclude that God's word is invulnerable

---

6.   Jorge Luis Borges, *Fervor de Buenos Aires* (Buenos Aires: Emecé, 1969).

7.   Steven Matthews, "Jorge Luis Borges: Fiction and Reading," *Ariel* 6 (Spring 1989): 63.

8.   Matthews, "Jorge Luis Borges," 66; emphasis added.

to the shifting prisms of time, change, language, and culture. Yet a Latter-day Saint understanding of revelation embraces the ironies and accents of changing context because of the way in which the dialectic between God's revealed word and human beings' mimetic word ignites a process of ongoing revelation. The novelty of revelation, from the Latter-day Saint perspective, is not just dependent on God's will and his intercession in the human cultural context through prophets; it is dependent also on every reader, who in what Anthony Cascardi calls the "adjectival moments of thought" marks with his own accent of interpretation new meanings of the Word.[9] Indeed, it is precisely this refraction of God's word caused by the contingencies of our reading moment that generates the need for a new revelation that we make possible by faithful reading. But this is not an argument for a free-for-all, every reader for himself. What exposes the differences between contexts and therefore the deeper meanings of new readings isn't an insistence on absolute relativism but paradoxically *the desire to see the sacred word's meaning as the same for all time and all places*. Without that desire to read attentively and devotedly and bring old words and phrases into the new context of our lives, we wouldn't see the gap between earthly meaning and heavenly truth. However, without an acceptance of the inevitable distance between our understanding and God's, without an abdication of the claim to know the mind of God precisely and completely, we would stand no chance of advancing in our understanding of truth. This is because we would always assume that our current understanding of God is sufficient. I suspect that such an assumption is part of what it means to worship a God after our own image.

---

9.   Anthony J. Cascardi, "Mimesis and Modernism," in *Literary Philosophers: Borges, Calvino, Eco*, ed. Jorge J. E. Gracia, Carolyn Korsmeyer, and Rodolphe Gasché (New York: Routledge, 2002), 123.

CONFIRMATIONS FROM 3 NEPHI

So what does this discussion have to do with 3 Nephi, as my title suggests it must? Critics and defenders of the Book of Mormon have tended to divide along the lines described above, that is, into polar opposite definitions of the sacred and secular. Arguably, this is because the book seems to ask us to conclude one of two things. On the one hand, we might conclude that the Book of Mormon is the work of a human being and is therefore in need of a radical historicization that would expose its human authorship, by Joseph Smith. We might read it, in other words, merely as Joseph's psychology and his moment in time writ large. The book might also delude the believing reader by becoming nothing more than her psychology and her moment of time writ large. This explains the search for the nineteenth-century context evident in the text and the accusation that believing readers are just projecting their own will onto the text. On the other hand, however, we might be tempted to argue alternatively that the Book of Mormon stands merely and always outside time and history, a narrative that comes from the heavens without the taint of circumstance, such that every believing reader is given, by means of passive reception, the entirety of its transcendence. This second conclusion, of course, places the book in a category entirely apart from all other books, even from the Bible, since it is not as vulnerable to the degradations of time and the hand of man. I would argue that coming to either of these conclusions alone is a mistake; the book offers itself as an enigma, a fusion of two seemingly impossible choices. A reading that combines devotion to God's Word with the creative energies of interpretation reveals textual structures that make us into Menardian readers. In this way a third possibility emerges that resolves the apparent enigma.

For a sacred work of literature, the Book of Mormon is unusually preoccupied with its own historicity and textuality, and yet it seems that a great number of its believing readers fail to acknowledge the relevance of *our* historicity as readers. That is, we are reluctant to consider how our cultural and historical circumstances have shaped our understandings of the book's textual meanings, and we are defensive about the relevance of New World history itself or nineteenth-century America to its meaning. The trump card that too often serves to dismiss concerns about the truthfulness or falseness of the book's historicity is the claim to revelation—as if revelation could render questions of historical contingency irrelevant. Such a view of revelation assumes that God can speak to us and transmit perfectly the meaning of his ahistorical position beyond our earthly realm into our particular circumstances; it is, in other words, to imagine a God who is inherently intolerant of or apart from human history. Alternatively, the book's disbelieving readers argue that its meaning can be reduced to the story of Joseph Smith's time, his psychology, or that it is at least rendered meaningless by the most recent claims of historians. Such an approach, to put it bluntly, replaces God with the historian as the one voice who stands outside time and orders chaos into meaning without accountability. In the former case, the reader treats the narrative's claims of historical origins as untouchable, paradoxically above history but ultimately determinative of the text's truth; we escape our historical condition categorically because of revelation, and the only salvation is to know as much of God's word as possible. In the latter case, the reader treats the historian's construction of the past as sacred, as the untouchable, unquestioned determinative source of the text's meaning; all knowledge, in other words, can be reduced to our historical condition, and the only salvation is to know as much history as possible. But both readers would seem to miss one of the central paradoxes of

Christ, which lies at the very heart of what revelation means: that God is revealed *in mortal flesh* as our brother, that his eternal and life-giving words come to us from a particular moment in time and space and language. That is, Christ's meaning as Savior is, in the more mundane sense of the word, *a translated being.* He has translated himself into our human context to make himself understood, but we must still translate him again, reread him as it were, so as to establish the grounds of his relevance to our individual lives.

The inherent ambiguity of transcendence as always grounded on the earth and never entirely free of the contingencies of human context seems oxymoronic and often proves too much for believers and nonbelievers alike.

So let us ask, What if the meaning of revelation is always instantiated by a particular moment in time and place, and what if its meaning receives another layer from each encounter by a new reader? Would this mean that revelation becomes purely secular and historicized every time? Or might this merely signify that revelation is perpetually necessary, that our failures to finally and completely transcend our historical circumstances open a window that grants glimpses of the mind of God as so much more broad, profound, and universal than our own feeble minds can conceive? This glimpse into heaven requires our obedience and submission to the portion of God's truth we have been given, but not because this portion is all there is or all that we will receive; rather, it is because the frontiers of truth remain open and subject to further rereadings, illuminations, and iterations. It is certainly true that the inherent ambiguity of such a view of transcendence as always grounded on the earth and never entirely free of the contingencies of human context seems oxymoronic and often proves too much for believers and nonbelievers alike. It is not dismissive of the legitimacy of U.S.-based readings of the Book of Mormon to suggest that we can anticipate revolutions in our understanding of the book when it is read by generations of Africans, Muslims, or Chinese. This is because such a theology places a degree of responsibility for interpretation that most readers would prefer to abdicate: the responsibility Oliver Cowdery faced when he was instructed to "study . . . out in [his] mind" (Doctrine and Covenants 9:8) what God might be saying. Let us remember that these words he sought to translate were written in a language he could not read. The Lord is calling for his imagination, his personality, his mind. Moreover, the Lord tells us that when he speaks, he speaks in order to correct us, "in [our] weakness, after the manner of [our] language, that [we] might come to understanding" (Doctrine and Covenants 1:24).

It is hard not to hear the hint that even divine language is not merely the transfer of information but a poetic reformation of a higher idea. A common distinction in literary criticism is made between poetic language that recognizes its own limitations and weaknesses (and thus opens us up to new possibilities of meaning) and propagandist language that seeks to hide its origins and contingencies in order to close down such possibilities. The great American author Toni Morrison, for example, in her 1993 Nobel Prize acceptance speech, praises Lincoln's Gettysburg Address for liberating rather than controlling or limiting meaning by its use of poetic strategies:

Refusing to monumentalize, disdaining the "final word," the precise "summing up," acknowledging their "poor power to add or
detract," his words signal deference to the uncapturability of the
life it mourns. It is the deference that moves [us], that recognition
that language can never live up to life once and for all. Nor should
it. Language can never "pin down" slavery, genocide, war [or for
that matter the mind and will of God]. Nor should it yearn for the
arrogance to be able to do so. Its force, its felicity is in its reach
toward the ineffable.[10]

Morrison's words here ring true. At the same time, unfortunately, and perhaps in response to the intolerance and dogmatism of many forms of belief, she gives religious language as one
of several examples of a language that, instead of acknowledging
its weakness, seeks to limit and control in ways not unlike the
language of political and commercial propaganda.

Of course, Morrison's criticism of religious language is not
uncommon. Indeed, it is usually assumed that religious faith is
inconsistent with tolerance, patience, humility, and self-questioning or open-mindedness and that sacred texts do not exhibit
these humble and poetic qualities of language. This is certainly
not the sense one has from the Book of Mormon, however, and
here I return again to 3 Nephi. Think of arguably one of the
most sacred moments of the book when Jesus prays for those in
his presence and the hearers do not bear witness to the words
he spoke but rather to their ineffable and undeniable power
(3 Nephi 17:15–17). The most explicit, literal, physical evidence
of God's love for humankind in a new continent, this prayer is
arguably the very heart of what the Book of Mormon witnesses,
and yet notice—after so much narrative, preaching, and prophe-
sying—the emphatic denial of the capacity of any human sense

---

10. Toni Morrison, "Nobel Lecture," December 7, 1993, *Georgia Review* 49,
   no. 1 (Spring 1995): 321.

to capture the essence of God's love for humankind that must remain beyond language:

> The eye hath never seen, neither hath the ear heard, before, so great and marvelous things as we saw and heard Jesus speak unto the Father; and no tongue can speak, neither can there be written by any man, neither can the hearts of men conceive so great and marvelous things as we both saw and heard Jesus speak; and no one can conceive of the joy which filled our souls at the time we heard him pray for us unto the Father. (3 Nephi 17:16–17)

That critics such as Morrison have ignored the essential humility and poetry of revealed scripture is perhaps a reaction to the arrogant triumphalism of many believers, but it is also the shortcoming of contemporary criticism itself, which often thinks about the sacred with no more nuance than the most fundamentalist believer. Paul Ricoeur is a critic who is an exception to this rule, however. He points to a particularly important feature of sacred texts that implicitly, if not explicitly, acknowledges the text's own partiality and its dependence on readers for the text to expand and magnify its meaning and to realize therefore its potential universality. Ricoeur points to the sacred text's capacity to imagine its own poetic force and the consequent need for a semiotic approach, as opposed to a historical-critical method, so as to consider the paradox of the text's simultaneous resistance to history and yet dependence on a fleshly reading that is instantiated in a particular place and time. As noted in chapter 10 herein, revelation, for Ricoeur, is the moment of transfer from the seeming ahistorical space of a sacred meaning to our history. It might be akin to what Nephi means when he asks us to "liken" the scriptures to ourselves (1 Nephi 19:24). This readerly "metaphorizing the narrative" displaces or relocates the text's meaning in the reader's capacity to imagine the figural nature of the text.[11] In other words, when we liken the scriptures to our circumstances, we allegorize them, we render them figural. This is not in defiance of their literal meaning or their historicity, or in denial of previous attributed meanings, but it is a way of layering a story's or a passage's meaning to extend across multiple circumstances. We might consider the way Nephi models this in his rereading of Isaiah as an example of new interpretations that make of the words of Isaiah a kind of Borgesian palimpsest, since we can simultaneously see the meaning of the words for Isaiah's time, for Nephi's time, and now for ours.

> Wresting the scriptures can happen when a reader forgets or ignores her own role in allegorizing sacred words for personal meaning, as if the personal meaning accounts for the totality of meaning contained in sacred writ.

We should worry that a purely reader-response theory of revelation defeats the very purpose of revelation; it gives license to the reader to imagine whatever the reader desires God's will to be. The sacred text becomes a mirror, saying back to us only what we already wanted to find, rather than a window through which we might peer to catch glimpses into the mind of God. This, I think, is what is meant by "wresting" the scriptures "unto [our] own destruction" (2 Peter 3:16; see also Doctrine and Covenants 10:63; Alma 13:20). But a faithful reading must

---

11. Paul Ricoeur, *Figuring the Sacred: Religion, Narrative, and Imagination,* trans. David Pellauer, ed. Mark I. Wallace (Minneapolis, MN: Fortress Press, 1995), 159.

engage in a seeming contradiction. It must admit the likelihood of self-deception and therefore abdicate the need for total identification with the scriptures even as it attempts to liken them to one's circumstances. The apparent contradiction is that a faithful reading imagines a voice speaking to us *in* our circumstances and yet coming from *beyond* them. I would thus suggest that wresting the scriptures can happen when a reader forgets or ignores her own role in allegorizing sacred words for personal meaning, as if the personal meaning accounts for the totality of meaning contained in sacred writ. *It is a failure to recognize the provisional and partial nature of the truths we harvest from reading.* Only the humility that is sufficient to receive the confirmations of the Spirit, which of course is key to faithful reading, is also sufficient to acknowledge its own partiality.

Wresting the word of God, of course, is a real possibility every time we read, and this is because there is no way to escape categorically the human conditions that limit our understanding. To come back to 3 Nephi, in perhaps one of the most fascinating and chastening moments in the Book of Mormon, an incident with the devastating consequence of rendering the New World unknown to the Old and rendering the significance of Christ's suffering and ascension to the limited geography of the Mediterranean and Europe, Christ explains to his New World audience that it is because of "stiffneckedness and unbelief they understood not my word" when he speaks of the other sheep (3 Nephi 15:18). He even goes so far as to suggest that it is "because of their iniquity that they know not of you" (v. 19). One has to consider the hard doctrine here. Given what we know about how limited the West's understanding was of the planet before 1492 and how common and easy it was for them to imagine they alone were at the center of all that was known of the world, what kind of wild and creative imaginings would it have required for Christ's disciples to conceive that he might be going to other peoples on other unknown continents? Perhaps the same kind of imagination Oliver Cowdery needed to study out in his mind a language he couldn't read? Even Columbus, the one man stubborn and erroneous enough to imagine he could travel from Spain to Japan in a matter of six weeks and therefore eligible for the task of connecting the continents, never understood the meaning of his own discovery. And yet Christ calls a staid and predictable understanding of the world, dictated by our moment in history and our geographical place and unable to imagine or ask about what we might not yet know, a form of iniquity! Revelation is his effort to pull us along, one step at a time, to get us beyond these limitations, and yet he also understands that he can reveal himself to us only in the vocabulary of our current understanding. So it would seem that revelation, although bringing new understanding, also potentially comes with vestiges of misunderstanding that we must work assiduously to dust off of his eternal Word. His Old World disciples interpreted the other sheep as the Gentiles, an interpretation indicating a major leap of understanding for them, a new and surprising awareness of the universality of Christ's atonement—and yet one that fell well short of a more truly global understanding of Christ's mission!

So wresting the scriptures is perhaps not even always a separate act from likening them to ourselves. We might ask why it is not inevitable that all readers, good and bad, will be hindered by the inherent "weakness" of their "language," by the contingencies of their historicity as human beings in finite and particular bodies, times, and places. It would seem we are back in the same position of having to choose between an interpretation of the meaning of a sacred text as merely and completely determined by an agency beyond our historical condition or merely and completely determined by that condition. If there is no middle ground between these two extreme positions, it is not possible to insist on a difference between good and bad readings, something I have been suggesting that crude reader-response theory and crude historicist readings of the Book of Mormon alike don't know how to do. Revelation may come even in the midst of our misunderstandings, which is perhaps one reason why Paul describes our mortal condition as looking through a glass darkly (see 1 Corinthians 13:12). We see, but we are also blinded. This might not satisfy our yearnings for the clouds of confusion and contention to finally clear, but it does at least make faith and imagination necessary, which also importantly makes us more accountable for the knowledge we gain. Reading is a moral activity, interpretation involves moral risk, and this is because knowledge isn't passively received but actively desired, imagined, hoped for, and finally grasped. The question then becomes: If an investment of so much of ourselves is required to gain a knowledge of God, how do we move closer to the mind of God and avoid the risk of self-projection and self-delusion?

THIRD NEPHI AS MENARDIAN PARADOX

Borges suggested, as we have seen, that it is the moment of coincidence between the same words in the mind of a reader and the mind of an author that reveals the inherent anachronism of all readings. And perhaps a Menardian paradox can be found right in 3 Nephi.[12] That Christ's Sermon on the Mount from the book of Matthew is repeated in 3 Nephi would seem to rather deliberately suggest this paradox, since the nearly identical words are

---

12. I originally gave a shorter version of this paper in 2008 at a conference on 3 Nephi sponsored by Brigham Young University's Neal A. Maxwell Institute for Religious Scholarship. Subsequently, I was surprised to discover in Grant Hardy's 2010 book, *Understanding the Book of Mormon*, that he makes the same connection between Borges and the Sermon on the Mount as set forth in 3 Nephi. See Grant Hardy, *Understanding the Book of Mormon* (New York: Oxford University Press, 2010), 194.

produced by Christ under different circumstances. One meaning of the repetition could be that his teachings and truth are entirely independent of context. (What else can be concluded from the fact that we find such precise repetition in two places in scripture?) Another, for the book's critics, is that the book is merely mimetic, derivative, and anachronistic. (Why does Christ use similar figural language from the Old World in a new context? If this is an authentic account of a historical visit to a new continent, why does he speak of swine and gods, bread and wine, when he might have invoked, say, agoutis and iguanas, or maize and chicha or pulque?) But I want to point to a third possibility, visible in light of Borges's short story.

As I indicated at the outset of this essay, there are important and subtle discrepancies between the sermon in Matthew and in 3 Nephi; the coincidence between the two accounts is only momentary, and the differences often point to new and richer meanings. However, I am here more concerned with how the considerable overlap between the biblical and Book of Mormon accounts might offer new and richer understanding. As J. Hillis Miller has argued, when two accounts of the same event are rendered and the differences no matter how small emerge, we become aware of a *third* text that lies above the two accounts. Miller insists that an ethics of reading begins with a recognition that every text responds to some "thing" that "demands it be respected by being put in words."[13] That "thing" can never be finally summed up in language because to try to do so is simply to repeat the problem by displacing that "thing" once more. Every text, then, "only gives itself. It hides its matter or thing as much as it reveals it. . . . It is unfaithful to the thing, by being

---

13. Joseph Hillis Miller, *The Ethics of Reading: Kant, de Man, Eliot, Trollope, James, and Benjamin* (New York: Columbia University Press, 1987), 105.

what it is, just these words on the page."[14] Repetition, in other words, highlights the textuality of words and the "thing" that is yet to be summed up. Without denying its own revelatory power, this mechanism renders language poetic.

This is perhaps akin to the so-called law of witnesses: two or three witnesses together point simultaneously to their own partiality and to a reality beyond them precisely because they coincide *and* diverge. What I mean to suggest is that in offering hints of richer understanding of Christ's words from Matthew or Luke, the sermon in 3 Nephi further discloses a gap between what is revealed and what God knows. Even though we don't have unlimited access to the latter, the textuality these discrepancies highlight models for us an understanding of revelation that lessens our tendency to wrest the scriptures to our own destruction. We might remember that, after teaching us of the iniquity of the Old World in failing to understand the meaning of "other sheep," Christ teaches us of *yet other* sheep (see 3 Nephi 16:1). Perhaps we are thus guided toward a radical openness of what is yet to be revealed, since we can now see how partial the Book of Mormon itself is, despite its own marvelous restorations. Like the disciples in the Old World or like Oliver Cowdery, we are chastened to imagine worlds beyond our own.

Allow me to return to a point made in the previous chapter. I insisted that, based on Ricoeur's understanding, *a good reading is a response to a semiotic pattern already established in the text whereby metaphors are narrativized.*[15] In addition to the example I gave previously of Lehi's journey into the wilderness and the various ways in which that story has been metaphorized by contemporary readers, we might also consider Alma's parable of the seed as a similar example, since it is clear that Alma's allegory

---

14. Miller, *Ethics of Reading*, 121.
15. Ricoeur, *Figuring the Sacred*, 159.

models for us how we ought to treat the very book we hold in our hands. It is for this reason, I argued, that we can find semiotic guidance from the Book of Mormon's overt textuality, its many allusions to itself as a mediated, made, and edited text, beginning with the very opening lines where Nephi announces his autobiography and declares, "I know that the record I make is true; and I make it with my own hand" (1 Nephi 1:3).

This textuality is especially apparent when we encounter a perfect coincidence of language in Matthew and 3 Nephi, a coincidence all the more self-consciously textual when we consider that the coincidence appears in translations into English

---

A theology of continuing revelation is radically committed to the value of individual will and the importance of individual context.

---

from apparently two different original languages—into a form of English, no less, that is antiquated for a contemporary reader. This is just one of many examples throughout the Book of Mormon of the book's almost brazen confession of its own textuality. Despite this overt textuality, however, critics act as if this textuality were some embarrassing facet the book seeks to hide behind its claim to authenticity. Even believing readers are often embarrassed or at least perplexed about these coincidences. I would suggest that the book's self-conscious textuality, what Ricoeur calls the "interpretive dynamism of the text itself" or its "interpretive function," is precisely the key to its interpretation and the key to escaping the false binaries into which so many of its readers fall.[16]

To quote Ricoeur again, he insists that "a theology that confronts the inevitability of the divine plan with the refractory nature of human actions and passions is a theology that engenders narrative."[17]

To the degree that the Book of Mormon anticipates this refractory nature of reading, it would seem to be a paradox, since there is anticipation of surprise or divine plan in unpredictability, but this is a paradox that foments the live nature of the text, that sustains its dynamism as part of a theology of continuing revelation. A theology of continuing revelation, in other words, is radically committed to the value of individual will and the importance of individual context. What is always yet to be, then, is not only future restoration of meaning but the next reader to join the adoption into Abraham's family. Reading and interpretation do not rest at some transcendent or ahistorical state but instead point us always back to the ground trod by each reader in time and space. This is a theology that is inherently hermeneutical, suggesting that its revelatory truths depend on the imagination to unlock and perpetuate their transcendence in the physical particularities of each human reader. As a hermeneutics in which the mortal context is always interpolated so as to be potentially sanctified, in which the earthly and secular are not separable but instead essential to the unveiling of divine pattern, we might call this an inherently Christian religion: "Christian" because it is Christ who offers himself as a translated being, the Word of God made flesh; and "religion" because, as the word implies, it requires and valorizes our perpetual rereadings of that Word.

---

16. Ricoeur, *Figuring the Sacred*, 161, 181.
17. Ricoeur, *Figuring the Sacred*, 182.

The Grace of
Nothingness

"Pray as if everything depends on the Lord.
Act as if everything depends on you."

Latter-day Saints recognize this adage as coming from Brigham Young, while Catholics attribute it to St. Augustine. In either case, I have never heard commentary on the strange duality of mind this "as if" theology requires, as if true faith requires remaining open to both possibilities simultaneously.

To act as if everything depends on us is to assume ultimate responsibility for the world, to accept the fact that we live in a universe of comprehensive accountability where all effects have causes and all causes have effects and where the link between them is always human choice. It also means we accept the possibility that God's intervention may never come or may come in

---

This essay is a slightly expanded version of an essay that appeared online at *Square Two* 6, no. 1 (Spring 2013), http://squaretwo.org/Sq2ArticleMiller SymposiumHandley.html. Reprinted here with permission.

a form that will not be to our liking. This existentialist stance is the great energizer of human choice and is vital to the self-made mythos of American life.

To pray as if everything depends on the Lord, on the other hand, is to recognize the limits of our ability to control or direct consequences; it is to assume the wisdom of a Hindu adage that

> ## Since it is fair to say that consequences never follow exactly as we plan, we set ourselves up for the feeling of betrayal, as if we had been deceived by the promise of a reliable, sequential ordering of life.

I often heard my former mentor, Lowell Bennion, recite: "To action alone hast thou a right, not to its fruits."[1] It is, in short, to recognize that while we can assume there is a relationship between cause and effect, we cannot presume to know what it is exactly. We can do good, but we cannot expect others, with their own agency, to respond to the good we do in the way that we want or expect. And when good does result, as Paul expresses, it is God who gives the "increase"; it is grace, not our own labors, that determines outcomes (1 Corinthians 3:6).

Adam Miller, in his book *Rube Goldberg Machines: Essays in Mormon Theology*, suggests that somehow Latter-day Saint mythology (and perhaps American mythology too) has been too

---

1. Mary Lythgoe Bradford, *Lowell L. Bennion: Teacher, Counselor, Humanitarian* (Salt Lake City: Signature Books, 1995), x.

impatient and has bypassed this requirement of a dual faith and created a kind of sacralized mythos of the self-made individual.[2] Work as hard as we can to be our best, and God will provide whatever it is we still lack to achieve perfection. Satisfaction guaranteed. The ultimate warranty on a perpetually breakable product. The problem this creates is that when things do not go as planned, we have to assume someone bears human responsibility, and so we go seeking the culprit. We can forget the fact that, as the Preacher tells us in Ecclesiastes, "the race is not to the swift, nor the battle to the strong, . . . but time and chance happeneth to them all" (Ecclesiastes 9:11).

By itself the existential disposition sponsors an urgency to act, but it also inspires delusions of human control and autonomy. By itself the prayerful disposition inspires acceptance of what is, but it also inspires indifference in the face of evil and suffering. Neither disposition can explain why we should concern ourselves with living according to principles or even commandments if they cannot guarantee the consequences we anticipated. Since it is fair to say that consequences never follow exactly as we plan, we set ourselves up for the feeling of betrayal, as if we had been deceived by the promise of a reliable, sequential ordering of life. Paul's emphasis on Christ's grace that enables this vital and fragile balancing act is instructive: "Not that I speak in respect of want: for I have learned, in whatsoever state I am, therewith to be content. I know both how to be abased, and I know how to abound: every where and in all things I am instructed both to be full and to be hungry, both to abound and to suffer need. I can do all things through Christ which strengtheneth me" (Philippians 4:11–13).

---

2. Adam S. Miller, *Rube Goldberg Machines: Essays in Mormon Theology* (Salt Lake City: Greg Kofford Books, 2012).

Perhaps for this reason Miller is correct to describe sinfulness as "failing to be where we are, to receive what is given, to *feel* what we are feeling."[3] It is a singular failure of faith to refuse to receive the conditions life imposes on us, for good or for ill. And such failure is as much a function of the mythos of absolute self-determination as it is of a kind of perpetual, resigned dependency on what we imagine to be the will of God. So maybe we should think further about this duality. Miller makes much of Christ's plea for the cup to pass and then his *nevertheless* that signifies a hard-earned submission. We might rephrase the adage: "Interpret the world as if God did not exist, and then interpret it as if he were everywhere." And in our suspension of judgment between these two possibilities, we will experience our limitations and lay hold of our possibilities while living less shackled by needless anxieties about what we can or cannot control and what we like or do not like about our lives. As the Reverend John Ames in Marilynne Robinson's *Gilead* affirms after a lifetime of unmet expectations and unresolved conflicts, "Existence is the essential thing and the holy thing."[4] This is the great wisdom of a Christian mind that no longer makes demands on God. The father in Terrence Malick's *The Tree of Life* was a man who once believed in the gospel of self-improvement. "You can't say, 'I can't,'" he tells his son. "You say, 'I'm having trouble. I am not done yet.'" But after losing his job and after losing his son to apparent suicide, he makes himself available to grace: "I wanted to be loved," he says, "because I was great. A big man. I'm nothing. Look at the glory around us. Trees and birds. I lived in shame. I dishonored it all and didn't notice the glory. I'm a foolish man."[5]

---

3. Miller, *Rube Goldberg Machines*, 12.
4. Marilynne Robinson, *Gilead* (New York: Farrar, Straus, and Giroux, 2005), 189.
5. Terrence Malick, director, *The Tree of Life* (Cottonwood Pictures, 2011). I have written about this film and its connection to Dostoevsky in more

This phrase echoes Dostoevsky's masterful novel *The Brothers Karamazov*. Zosima tells the story of his own spiritual development by recounting the death of his brother, who died young, after passing from atheism to belief in God. As he was dying, his brother no longer feared death: "Why count the days, when even one day is enough for a man to know all happiness. My dears, why do we quarrel, boast before each other, remember each other's offenses? Let us go to the garden, let us walk and play and love and praise and kiss each other, and bless our life."[6] Malick's film attempts to portray in long, seemingly uneventful but tender scenes this kind of exultation in life itself, an exultation embodied in child's play and in the mother's joie de vivre. Zosima's brother stares outside the window on his deathbed, exulting in the trees and birds. "None of us could understand it then, but he was weeping with joy: 'Yes,' he said, 'there was so much of God's glory around me: birds, trees, meadows, sky, and I alone lived in shame, I alone dishonored everything, and did not notice the beauty and glory of it all."[7] Dostoevsky's point here, certainly important to Malick, is that paradise can be here and now, but we must learn to love nature and exult in the chance to be alive, even if that means accepting the inevitability of terrible suffering. Zosima feels that no scripture is more telling of our human condition than the book of Job, because it tells the story of a man who accepts death and loss and the world's seeming indifference and yet serves and loves and worships God with integrity. Zosima says, "In the face of earthly

---

detail in "Faith, Sacrifice, and the Earth's Glory in Terrence Malick's 'The Tree of Life,'" *Angelaki: The Journal of the Theoretical Humanities* 19, no. 4 (Winter): 79–93.

6.   Fyodor Dostoevsky, *The Brothers Karamazov*, trans. Richard Pevear and Larissa Volokhonsky (New York: Farrar, Straus, and Giroux, 2002), 289.

7.   Dostoevsky, *Brothers Karamazov*.

truth, the enacting of eternal truth is accomplished."[8] This is to say we can find the deepest joys only in the midst of our greatest sorrows, that we can understand the gift of life only in the context of death and loss. Blessed are the hungry, the poor, those who know that they lack, says Jesus, for only in knowing our insufficiency and the goodness of God can we have the promise of fulfillment, which comes precisely in the recognition and acceptance of insufficiency. We err spiritually, in other words, and we do unspeakable harm to the world because we keep trying so hard to make ourselves self-sufficient, to be the "big man" Malick's father wanted to be.

Appreciation of life's glory comes at a cost: one must forsake a will to control and the expectation of a desired outcome. In other words, glory is possible only in a universe where beauty isn't seen as expected or even necessary. Malick's tree of life is not some iconic symbol of a lost past or a dreamed-of future but rather a symbol of the trees of the ordinary experience of this world. So in a sense, God is possible only in a universe where he doesn't appear to be necessary or where holiness would stand out as some kind of exception to the facts of physical life. To paraphrase Annie Dillard, to lay claim to God's existence is no less rational than trying to explain the bare fact of the extravagance of a giraffe.[9] If we imagine that the universe points to the necessity of God and therefore the inevitability of benevolent control of events, we are never confronted by the challenge of having to forge meaning freely. Belief becomes a genuine and courageous choice rather than mechanistically predetermined by order or logic. Freedom is possible, it seems, only in a universe of indeterminacy.

---

8. Dostoevsky, *Brothers Karamazov*, 292.
9. Annie Dillard, *Pilgrim at Tinker Creek* (New York: Harper Perennial, 1998), 146.

As Miller says, "In opening our hands to receive what [the present moment] offers and give what it requires, we must confess our dependence, our insufficiency, our lack of autonomy."[10] This is what he calls a kind of nonsequential grace. Malick's "glory" is the miracle of existence, a miracle visible only to those who experience life as a gift—which means to recognize life unconditionally, not as something earned, as something we measure

---

King Benjamin knew that anticipated temporal blessings are not guaranteed. But he has already specified what those blessings are: time, breath, physical life, judgment, and choice.

---

and assess according to our preferences and predilections, as something emanating from and shaped by our choices. Rather, the gift of life is something we recognize as far surpassing us and our understanding. It is more than whatever we might do to life with our pitifully insufficient accounting. King Benjamin in the Book of Mormon insists that such humility is the engine of atoning healing:

> I say unto you that if ye should serve him who has created you from the beginning, and is preserving you from day to day, by lending you breath, that ye may live and move and do according to your own will, and even supporting you from one moment to another—I say, if ye should serve him with all your whole souls yet

---

10. Miller, *Rube Goldberg Machines*, 10.

ye would be unprofitable servants. And behold, all that he requires of you is to keep his commandments; and he has promised you that if ye would keep his commandments ye should prosper in the land; and he never doth vary from that which he hath said; therefore, if ye do keep his commandments he doth bless you and prosper you. (Mosiah 2:21–22)

The blessings are immediate, he says. What can he mean by this? Surely he knew, as did his people, that good people often suffer, that anticipated temporal blessings are not guaranteed, that we cannot bind the Lord. But he has already specified what those blessings are: time, breath, physical life, judgment, and choice. God's grace, as Miller has it, "is the substance of life" itself and is therefore, like the Preacher's notion of time and chance, nonsequential.[11] It is merely our biology. To be dust is perhaps shameful, but only in the existential sense, not because of anything we have or haven't done. In King Benjamin's terms, it is to be "dust," to be a "beggar." It is to understand our own "nothingness, and his goodness and long-suffering towards [us], unworthy creatures" (Mosiah 4:2, 19, 11). Creatures. Created beings. Undeserving because we are not autonomous but *made*, and made *interdependent*. But unlike shame born of sin, this shame inspires awe, gratitude, and fullness in the face of life's magnificence. This is the great lesson of Job. Though worms will eat him, though he is dust, he knows he will see God in the flesh. Though life distorts the meaning of his life into a farce, it has transcendent value. Theologian William Brown writes of Job's creation account as offering no "cozy cosmos" but rather one that "is terrifyingly vast and alien."[12] Brown notes: "Job comes to realize

---

11.   Miller, *Rube Goldberg Machines*, 9.
12.   William Brown, *The Seven Pillars of Creation: The Bible, Science, and the Ecology of Wonder* (New York: Oxford University Press, 2010), 129.

that the world does not revolve around himself, nor even around humanity. Creation is polycentric."[13] This exposure to previously unimagined diversity and immensity tempers Job. He must come to accept that he, like all of creation, is an alien, not central, but also free. He learns to "to revel in his freedom, wild thing that he is, and to step lightly on God's beloved, vibrant Earth."[14]

The mythos of the self-made individual is, according to Miller, a narrative. It is a story of cause and effect, a linear sequencing of human existence that stresses the arithmetic of choice, of human cause and human effect. But what if we must confess, as it appears we all must, that there is no mastery of consequences, no formula by which we control or dictate outcome? What if we must say, with Malick's father, that we have been foolish in thinking we could? Does this mean that choices don't matter? No. As Job discovered, integrity is forged in the cauldron of life when experienced as a series of non sequiturs. Jesus said repeatedly that the true test of obedience and love was precisely when they made the least sense—loving enemies, praying in secret, knowing not what the hands are doing, losing—not finding—oneself. All it requires is that we must lose that maniacal and selfish need for life's plotline and instead fall in love with life as a plotless poem. Then in finding life out of sequence, we also find that love and grace—like all good metaphors—inspire immeasurable gratitude precisely because they are gifts, neither necessary nor inevitable. We should pray to be so fortunate.

---

13. Brown, *Seven Pillars of Creation*, 133.
14. Brown, *Seven Pillars of Creation*, 140.

Index

About the Author

G eorge Handley teaches interdisciplinary humanities at Brigham Young University, where he also serves as the associate director of the Faculty Center. He received his BA from Stanford University and his MA and PhD in comparative literature at UC Berkeley. His scholarly publications and creative writing focus on the intersection between religion, literature, and the environment. His most recent books include the memoir *Home Waters: A Year of Recompenses on the Provo River*, a collection of essays entitled *Learning to Like Life: A Tribute to Lowell Bennion*, and the novel *American Fork*.